1908 Edvard Munch *The Scream* Franz Marc *Little Blue Horse* Ernst Barla... Self-
...launay *Nude Woman Reading* Jackson Pollock *Lavender Mist* Piet Mond... ... Yellow
...ol *Double Elvis* Roy Lichtenstein *Stepping Out* Banksy *Flower* Roa *Birds* ... Edgar
...arc *Little Blue Horse* Ernst Barlach *The Destitution* Frida Kahlo *Self-portrait ... ...ey* Pablo Picasso
...llock *Lavender Mist* ... ... Aubrey Beardsley *How Sir Bedivere Cast*
Out Banksy *Flower* ... *Birds* Claude Monet *Water-Lily Pond* Edgar Degas *Dancers at the Barre* Peder Severin
...tution Frida Kahlo *Self-portrait with Small Monkey* Pablo Picasso *Portrait of Dora Maar* Vincent van Gogh *Self-*
...on with Blue and Yellow* Aubrey Beardsley *How Sir Bedivere Cast the Sword Excalibur into the Water* Saul Bass
...ater-Lily Pond* Edgar Degas *Dancers at the Barre* Peder Severin Kroyer *Summer Evening Skagen, 1908* Edvard
...onkey* Pablo Picasso *Portrait of Dora Maar* Vincent van Gogh *Self-portrait as a Painter* Robert Delaunay *Nude*
...ow Sir Bedivere Cast the Sword Excalibur into the Water* Saul Bass *Bonjour Tristesse* Andy Warhol *Double Elvis*
...rre* Peder Severin Kroyer *Summer Evening Skagen, 1908* Edvard Munch *The Scream* Franz Marc *Little Blue Horse*
...t van Gogh *Self-portrait as a Painter* Robert Delaunay *Nude Woman Reading* Jackson Pollock *Lavender Mist* Piet
...r Saul Bass *Bonjour Tristesse* Andy Warhol *Double Elvis* Roy Lichtenstein *Stepping Out* Banksy *Flower* Roa *Birds*
...908 Edvard Munch *The Scream* Franz Marc *Little Blue Horse* Ernst Barlach *The Destitution* Frida Kahlo *Self-*
...elaunay *Nude Woman Reading* Jackson Pollock *Lavender Mist* Piet Mondrian *Composition with Blue and Yellow*
...ol *Double Elvis* Roy Lichtenstein *Stepping Out* Banksy *Flower* Roa *Birds* Claude Monet *Water-Lily Pond* Edgar
...arc *Little Blue Horse* Ernst Barlach *The Destitution* Frida Kahlo *Self-portrait with Small Monkey* Pablo Picasso
...llock *Lavender Mist* Piet Mondrian *Composition with Blue and Yellow* Aubrey Beardsley *How Sir Bedivere Cast*
Out Banksy *Flower* Roa *Birds* Claude Monet *Water-Lily Pond* Edgar Degas *Dancers at the Barre* Peder Severin
...tution Frida Kahlo *Self-portrait with Small Monkey* Pablo Picasso *Portrait of Dora Maar* Vincent van Gogh *Self-*
...ion with Blue and Yellow* Aubrey Beardsley *How Sir Bedivere Cast the Sword Excalibur into the Water* Saul Bass
...ater-Lily Pond* Edgar Degas *Dancers at the Barre* Peder Severin Kroyer *Summer Evening Skagen, 1908* Edvard
...onkey* Pablo Picasso *Portrait of Dora Maar* Vincent van Gogh *Self-portrait as a Painter* Robert Delaunay *Nude*
...ow Sir Bedivere Cast the Sword Excalibur into the Water* Saul Bass *Bonjour Tristesse* Andy Warhol *Double Elvis*
...rre* Peder Severin Kroyer *Summer Evening Skagen, 1908* Edvard Munch *The Scream* Franz Marc *Little Blue Horse*
...t van Gogh *Self-portrait as a Painter* Robert Delaunay *Nude Woman Reading* Jackson Pollock *Lavender Mist* Piet
...r Saul Bass *Bonjour Tristesse* Andy Warhol *Double Elvis* Roy Lichtenstein *Stepping Out* Banksy *Flower* Roa *Birds*
...908 Edvard Munch *The Scream* Fra... ...ach *The Destitution* Frida Kahlo *Self-*
...t Delaunay *Nude Woman Reading* J... ...Mondrian *Composition with Blue and*
...y Warhol *Double Elvis* Roy Lichtenstein ... Roa *Birds* Claude Monet *Water-Lily Pond*

Modern Art Adventures

First published in Great Britain in 2015 by
Modern Books, an imprint of Elwin Street Limited
3 Percy Street
London W1T 1DE
www.elwinstreet.com

Copyright © 2015 Elwin Street Limited

Conceived and produced by
Elwin Street Limited
3 Percy Street
London W1T 1DE
www.elwinstreet.com

The activities described in this book are to be carried out with parental supervision at all times. Every effort has been made to ensure the safety of the activities detailed. Neither the author nor the publishers shall be liable or responsible for any harm or damage done allegedly arising from any information or suggestion in this book.

ISBN: 978-1-906761-54-7

Original photography: Ian Garlick

Picture credits
Claude Monet, *The Water-Lily Pond*, Bridgeman Art Library/National Gallery, London, UK, 13 ; Edgar Degas, *Dancers at the Barre*, Alamy/PAINTING, 10, 19; Kroyer Peder Severin, *Summer Evening Skagen, 1908*, Bridgeman Art Library/Bonhams, London, UK, 25; Edvard Munch, *The Scream*, Alamy/Dennis Hallinan, 33; Franz Marc, *Little Blue Horse*, Bridgeman Art Library/Saarland Museum, Saarbrucken, Germany, 30, 39; Ernst Barlach, *The Destitution*, Alamy/INTERFOTO, 45; Frida Kahlo, *Self-portrait with Small Monkey*, Alamy/Vidura Luis Barrios, 53; Pablo Picasso, *Portrait of Dora Maar*, Alamy/Peter Barritt, 50, 59; Vincent van Gogh, *Self-portrait as a Painter*, The Bridgeman Art Library/De Agostini Picture Library, 65; Robert Delaunay, *Nude Woman Reading*, The Art Archive/Fine Art Museum Bilbao/Collection Dagli Orti, 73; Jackson Pollock, *Number 1, (Lavender Mist)*, Alamy/B Christopher, 70, 79; Piet Mondrian, *Composition with Blue and Yellow*, Alamy/B Christopher, 85; Aubrey Beardsley, *How Sir Bedivere Cast the Sword Excalibur into the Water*, The Bridgeman Art Library/Private Collection, 93; Saul Bass, *Bonjour Tristesse*, The Kobal Collection/Columbia, 90, 99; Andy Warhol, *Double Elvis*, Alamy/Peter Horree, 107; Roy Lichtenstein, *Stepping Out*, Alamy/Peter Horree, 104, 113; Banksy, *Flower*, Alamy/Derek Webb, 121; Roa, *Birds*, FatCap Agency, 118, 127.

Printed in China
5 4 3 2 1

Modern Art
Adventures

Over **35** Hands-on Art Projects Inspired by

Artists from Monet to Banksy

MAJA PITAMIC AND JILL LAIDLAW
Introduction by Rachel Ropeik, Museum of Modern Art

Contents

Introduction

'Make a swirling background . . . using shaving cream and paint.'
'Bring a little bit of nature and street art into your bedroom.'
'Do you want your picture to be "noisy" or "quiet"?'

I don't know about you, but these sound like fun to me: fun, accessible art projects for kids ages six and up inspired by 18 famous works of modern art. You might take these projects as a jumping-off point to reach your own creative heights. But no matter how you use this book, it will help you bring art to life with narratives, materials and instructions that are kid-friendly.

We need books like this. Too often, art – the kind by famous artists hanging in museums and the kind we can make in our own homes – is something we adults easily dismiss with familiar excuses like 'I'm not an artist' or 'I don't know anything about it' or 'I'm not very good at that'. When that self-deprecation is what we display to our kids at an early age, it becomes their self-deprecation, too.

What if, instead, art could be something that inspired family conversation and produced reactions like a proud 'We made that' or an eager 'Look what we can do'? As someone who has devoted my professional life to making art accessible to people from ages four to . . . quite a lot older than four, that's the kind of reaction I'm looking for. I want art to be fun and enjoyable without the intimidation factor.

That is exactly where this book can help. It includes an introduction to 18 famous artworks from the twentieth century up to the present and 36 hands-on projects that you and kids near and dear to you can do to bring those artists' styles to life at your own kitchen table. With *Modern Art Adventures,* your kids can be Pop artists, Abstract painters,

Impressionists, Expressionists, clever Illustrators, Portraitists, Street artists and more. No prior historical or artistic expertise required. It's all right here for you.

So put your artistic experimenting hats on. After all, that's what the modern artists featured in this book did: experiment. They played around to create entirely new styles and techniques. They each left their own unique stamp on the art world. That is what I tell the families I teach in museums. When I combine that with hands-on art-making like the projects you'll find here, kids (and adults, too) internalise the art they've seen and add their own unique stamps to it. It's a sure-fire recipe for engagement, empowerment and success.

Nothing is stopping you or the kids in your life from being artists. Let this book help you get started.

Rachel Ropeik is a Family Programmes Educator at the Museum of Modern Art and a Senior Museum Educator and Teacher Services Coordinator at the Brooklyn Museum.

How to use this book

Modern Art Adventures introduces both adults and children to works of modern art and uses those works to inspire related art activities. You don't need to know anything about art history, because everything is here for you: a short explanation of each painting, print or illustration is given. You also don't need to be able to draw, because the projects are simple, easy to follow and vary in their practice, from drawing to constructing, assembling and painting. With *Modern Art Adventures,* all you really need are children with enquiring minds and creative streaks.

The book is divided by key movements and styles in the history of modern art, starting with the groundbreaking Impressionists and moving through the twentieth century to contemporary Street artists. In addition to telling you the story of each work, we are trying to encourage you and your child to think about and discuss questions that will help you both expand your understanding of art. Every activity contains a detailed materials list, clear step-by-step instructions paired with photos and top tips from the authors.

To further enhance your adventures in modern art, at the back of the book you will find artist biographies, a helpful glossary of art-related terms, a list of museums where you can see the featured artworks in person and a 'Tools of the trade' page – where you can learn pointers that will help you make the most out of each activity.

This book evolves with your child; younger children may need assistance with the activities, but as they grow older they will be able to do the projects on their own, though we recommend that parents always supervise their kids when working with any sharp objects.

1 Impressionism

Impressionism was an art movement that gained prominence in the 19th century, started by a group of artists in Paris. The focus was on showing a visual impression of a particular moment — particularly the varying effects of light, colour and movement. For these artists, the word *impression* meant something or someone 'caught in a moment', undistinguished and undefined. The three artists for this chapter are Claude Monet, Edgar Degas and Peder Severin Kroyer. Each of these artists interpreted this 'caught in a moment' quality in their own personal style, and each took very different journeys through Impressionism. Interestingly, though, all three also arrived at the same journey's end — the edges of abstract art.

Water-Lily Pond

In his painting *Water-Lily Pond*, Claude Monet's signature brushstrokes and soft colour palette immerse the viewer in the verdant scenery of his water-lily pond in Giverny.

Artist	Claude Monet
Nationality	French
Painted	1899

What's the story?

Monet had the Japanese bridge and pond that feature in his painting *Water-Lily Pond* specially constructed for his garden in Giverny, France, to which he moved in the 1870s. But it is neither the bridge nor the water lilies that are the stars of the painting. 'The subject is not important to me; what I want to reproduce is what exists between the subject and me,' he said. For Monet this represented the capturing of atmosphere through the effects of light. This painting is one of 250 of the same subject all painted at different times of the day to capture the differing intensities of light.

Monet gave the movement its name with his painting entitled *Impression, Sunrise*. His early paintings, such as *Women in the Garden* (1866), contain clarity of light but make no attempt at capturing atmosphere. In his later paintings of the 1870s the clarity is lost as everything is filtered through the sunlight. Monet concerns himself not with the objects depicted but with the effect of the light on those objects, as is the case with the Japanese bridge. The bridge encloses and immerses us in the scene where water and water lily become blurred into a world of shimmering light. The water-lily series marked the end of Monet's exploration into Impressionism and takes us to the edges of Abstract art.

Think about . . .

Other artists besides Monet had chosen to work in the 'open air', but what was different in what Monet was trying to achieve with his work?
The clue is in the fact that Monet chose to paint 250 paintings of the same subject; it reveals a scientific empirical approach to observing the effects of light.

Water often features in Impressionist paintings. Why do you think this may be the case?
Think about the reflective nature of water and how it can bring an extra dimension to light.

Project: A fleeting impression

Monet painted at different times of the day to capture the differing light conditions. For this project we are going to work like Monet and sketch the same subject four times at different times of the day. If it is a cloudy day and you cannot see much contrast between light and shade, use a lamp and draw your four sketches by placing a lamp in different positions around your subject. We will use watercolour pencils, which are highly portable and have a lovely soft line.

1 Start your first sketch in the early morning on a sunny day. If you are not using a pad of paper, tape or clip your sheet of paper to your board or tabletop. Next to your board have your pencils and pot of water.

2 Using a pale-coloured pencil, start by lightly marking out the shape, height and width of your object. When you are happy with your markings, move onto defining the areas like the stem, flower and leaves.

3 Working from dark to light, build up the colour with quick, light strokes. Look in particular for areas of light and dark to achieve the best possible contrast. Where you have to cover larger areas turn the pencil onto its side and lightly shade the object in, noting the lighter and darker areas.

4 Go back over your drawing but this time use your waterbrush or a wet paintbrush so that the colours start blending together. Your completed drawing should take you no longer than 15 minutes. Space your other three drawings throughout the day and by the end of the day you will see the variations in light and shade.

Top tips

• Remember these are sketches – an impression is more important than accuracy. You could go on to create more detailed drawings.
• Experiment by using different media and techniques.

Project: Capturing the light

Before you start this next project, look really closely at Monet's painting and observe the colours he is using. From your observations choose your paint colours, which should include violets, greens, yellows and white, but no black. Instead of oil paint, which Monet used, you will be using acrylic paint, which creates a nice surface texture. Acrylic also has the advantage of being able to be immediately painted over if you're not happy with what you have created.

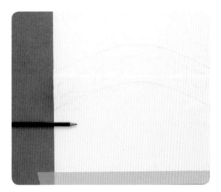

1 Cover your work area and then stick your sheet of paper down with masking tape. Using your pencil, mark out a bridge shape.

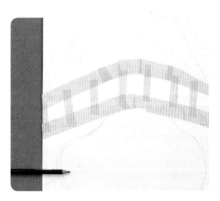

4 With your soft pencil, very lightly mark out the areas of trees and the pond.

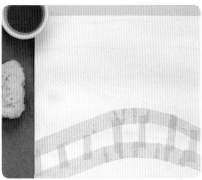

2 Cut pieces of masking tape and cover your bridge with it. Wet your sponge and sweep it across the page until it is covered and slightly damp.

3 Repeat, but this time load the sponge with blue watercolour paint or watered-down poster paint. All the paper should now be covered in a blue wash. Leave to dry.

You will need

An A4 or A3 sheet of watercolour paper

A board, book or protected tabletop to stick your paper on (optional)

Masking tape

Blue watercolour paint or watered-down poster paint

A sponge

A soft pencil

A pair of scissors

Acrylic paints in a Monet palette: violets, yellows, greens and white

A selection of brushes in various sizes, preferably square-ended

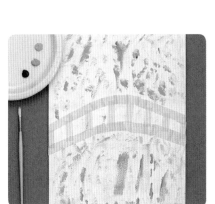

5 Take a dry brush and load it with a dark green paint. With a dabbing action apply the paint to the areas of foliage. Repeat with a different brush using a lighter shade of green. Allow the paint to dry before applying a new colour.

6 Keep applying the paint in this way, working from dark to light colours, leaving white until last. When the painting is dry, carefully peel off the masking tape bridge. You can choose to keep it white or add in the light and shade using the same painting technique.

Top tips

• Check your work by standing away from it to judge the effect.

• If you don't have any acrylic paint, use poster paint and mix in some white glue to thicken it. However, make sure you clean your brushes out right away.

Dancers at the Barre

In *Dancers at the Barre* we are struck by the 'snapshot' quality of the work. During this period of his life, Edgar Degas was increasingly influenced by the new science of photography and even more so by Japanese prints with their unconventional compositions that give the appearance of informality.

Artist	Edgar Degas
Nationality	French
Painted	1888

What's the story?

Despite exhibiting with the Impressionists and being a friend of Manet, Degas always remained detached from the rest of the Impressionists and could not be said to share the same understanding of art as, for example, Monet. So why is he included with the Impressionists? It's mainly because Degas's pictures have the quality of the 'snapshot'. Degas's world is the world of the ballet, races and café life. He sees with an unflinching eye life's beauty and its grimness.

In *Dancers at the Barre*, we seem to have caught the dancers mid-practice, with their backs turned towards us (a typical Degas device). The pastel strokes are so loose that it appears to be the work of a moment, but only an artist of supreme skill could capture this with such confidence. Similarly, the use of the hot orange against the cool blue of the dancers' skirts adds shimmering movement to the painting. But for all the supposed informality of the work, if you look at the positions of the dancers, they balance each other in perfect symmetry so that their bodies almost fuse together in an abstract shape. So for Degas reality is refined in order to capture life in 'its essential gestures'.

Think about . . .

How is the work of Degas different from Monet's?
Degas almost derided Monet's ideas of working in the open air to capture the effects of light. Degas's art, while giving the impression of a 'snapshot', is always composed to achieve its aim of capturing the essence of life. Despite taking very different pathways, both artists at the end of their artistic lives touched on the fringes of Abstract art.

Why were Japanese prints so influential in Western art during this period?
From about the 1860s Japanese prints became available in the West for the first time and such was their influence on western European art that the French coined the term *Japonisme*. The Impressionists were particularly struck by the compositional freedom that the prints offered and were quick to make use of it in their own works.

Project: Black and White

Dancers at the Barre is very striking in its use of colour but Degas's first studies were always in black and white. Like Degas you will use chalk, charcoal and photography to make figure studies.

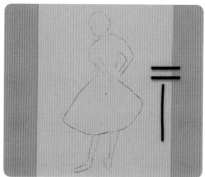

1 Start by taking some photos of your friends or choosing photos from a magazine – aim for unusual angles and dynamic poses. Select a photo and choose one figure from it. For our sketch we've taken inspiration directly from Degas.

2 Take a sheet of pastel paper or construction paper and a piece of charcoal and lightly mark out the proportions of the body. When you are happy with the proportions, define the body outline more clearly.

3 Fill in more details of the figure. Observe and decide which areas are going to be black, white and in-between tones. Keep your strokes loose and light, not forgetting the spaces surrounding your figure.

4 As in the Monet sketches this sketch should take you no longer than 15 minutes. For your next sketch you could try introducing another figure. Do as many sketches as you wish as it will help you in the next Degas project.

Top tips

• After you've finished your drawings, spray your sketches with a fixative or hairspray to prevent smudging.
• Black has special characteristics compared with other colours. It appears more intense in the background and less intense in the foreground. Degas uses it on the black ribbons of some of his dancers to give greater form to their figures.

Project: Mixing it up

In *Dancers at the Barre*, Degas uses a combination of cool blue and hot orange. For this next project you are going to use cool violet and hot yellow to see if this has the same impact. Like Degas you are also going to combine and mix different media. You will find this project easier if you have done the previous Degas project.

You will need

An A4 or A3 sheet of peach-coloured pastel paper or sugar paper

A small box of oil pastels

A graphite or black watercolour pencil

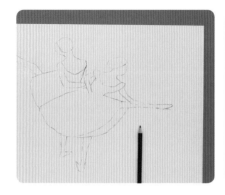

1 Using a copy of *Dancers at the Barre*, lightly sketch out your figures onto the paper using your graphite or watercolour pencil. When you are happy with the figures add more details.

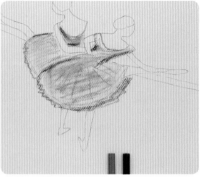

2 Take your violet-coloured pastel and lightly and loosely fill in the dancers' skirts and tops. If you don't have a violet pastel use pink and purple and then blend them together with your finger.

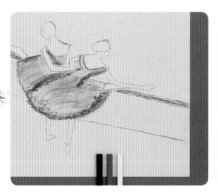

3 Now move on to filling in the background. Like the violet pastel, apply your hot-yellow pastel loosely and patchily so that some of the colour from the paper still shows through. If you place the pastel on its side the colour will not appear so intense.

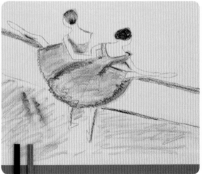

4 Next, with your other pastel colours, fill in the details on the bodies including the skin tones and hair. Finally, add the darkest black shadows and the white highlights. Look to see which parts of the body Degas defines in black.

Top tips

• Try using other hot and cold colours like red and green. Complementary colours appear particularly vibrant when placed alongside each other.

• If you have never used oil pastels before, experiment on a scrap piece of paper before. They can be easily blended together with your finger.

• Degas was the master of many types of media so try this project again and use different materials, like acrylics.

Summer Evening, Skagen, 1908

Peder Severin Kroyer's skilful blending techniques and atmospheric colour choices, as seen in his *Summer Evening, Skagen, 1908*, defined a whole movement of Danish painting and uplifted the Skagen area to near-heavenly heights by portraying it as an idyllic, elegant and romantic seaside destination.

Artist	Peder Severin Kroyer
Nationality	Danish
Painted	1908

What's the story?

We have come to regard Impressionism as being a French art movement, but there were artists across the world who were also experimenting with painting in the open air. Among these was a small group of Danish artists who set up an artists' colony on the coast of Jutland in an area called Skagen. These artists were drawn to this area because of the wonderful light, which was given the name 'blue light', so called because at certain times of the day the skyline and sea seemed to blur into a blue haze.

This is what we observe in *Summer Evening, Skagen, 1908*, painted by the leading artist of the Skagen painters, Peder Severin Kroyer. Using thickly applied oil paint he limits his palette to shades of blue and purple, which merge one into the other so that sea and sky are indistinguishable. The shoreline is simply indicated by a honey-coloured triangle at the right-hand corner of the painting. The triangle shape is echoed by the loosely painted single boat out on the horizon. The shape cuts across the horizontal pattern of the waves. Set against this tapestry of blues and purples is the glowing sun whose sinking reflection is caught in the white-tipped waves. The painting was made at the end of Kroyer's life and, like Monet and Degas before him, his journey of Impressionism had taken him towards the Abstract.

Think about . . .

What are the essential differences between the Skagen Impressionists and the French Impressionists?
While the Skagen painters were interested in the effects of light, this was combined with elements of realism, particularly for Kroyer, who went to Paris and studied under Léon Bonnat. In works such as *Fishermen Hauling the Net on Skagen's North Beach* (1882) Kroyer tries to capture the local fishermen, while in *St. John's Eve Bonfire on Skagen's Beach* (1906) he captures the local community.

How successful were the Skagen artists?
So successful were the Skagen artists in creating through their paintings a community that was simple but happy and bathed in a glorious light that people starting flocking to the area, and Skagen soon became a popular beach resort.

'This picture makes me feel peaceful.'

Kathy, age 8

Project: Dark into light

This project will help you to understand the nature of watercolour. It is advisable to do this project before you do the 'Hues of blue' project.

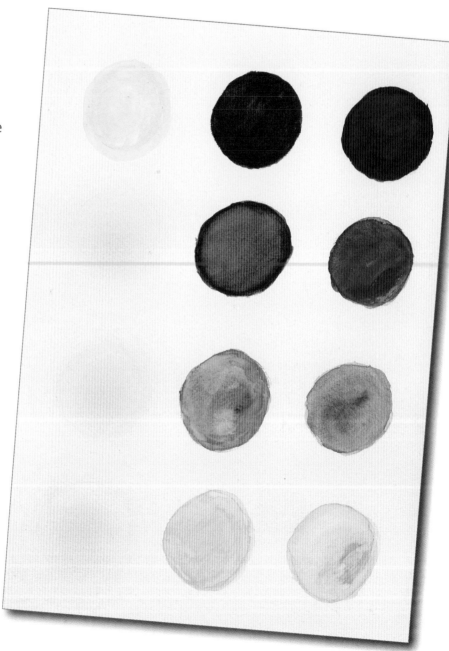

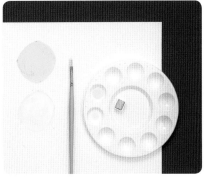

1 Begin by wetting your brush and loading it with the yellow watercolour paint. At the top left-hand corner of your sheet make a circle of yellow. This should be the most intense shade of yellow you can paint.

2 After cleaning your brush, wet it again, but this time water down the yellow paint. Test the intensity on your palette, and make a second circle under the first one. The second yellow circle should be one shade lighter in colour than the first circle.

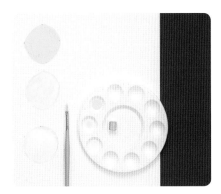

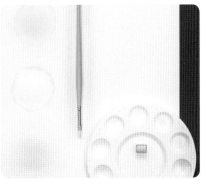

3 Repeat these steps, but this time water down the yellow watercolour further and make a third circle under the second. Again, this should be one shade lighter than the second circle.

4 Repeat these steps again to make a fourth circle, which should be a shade lighter than the third circle. Go on to repeat these steps with the red and blue paints.

Top tips

• See if you can match up the shades of colour throughout the yellow, red and blue.
• Don't forget to clean your brush between colours. This is what your second pot of water is for – to rinse your brush out. Once you have done this, flick your brush to remove excess water.

Project: Hues of blue

Kroyer used oil paint for his painting *Summer Evening Skagen, 1908*, but for this project you are going to use watercolours and a technique called 'wet on wet'. Watercolour paint is applied in layers to a wet colour wash, which allows the colours to bleed into each other, producing a beautiful blending effect that mimics Kroyer's.

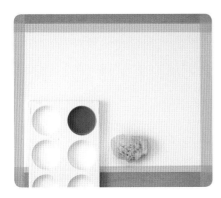

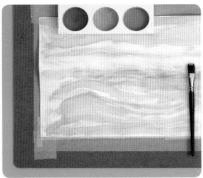

1 Stick your paper onto your board with the masking tape. Examine Kroyer's painting and look at the shade of blue used on the horizon. See if you can match that blue on your palette.

2 Wet your sponge, load it with the blue paint and cover the entire page. While the page is still wet, mix and apply the other blues and violets for the sea and sky using the square-headed brush.

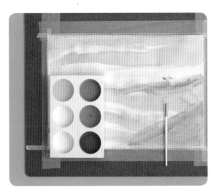

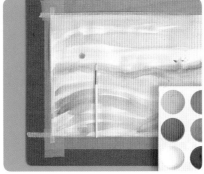

3 Wait until the paper is almost dry and then apply the finer details. First mix the honey-coloured paints and, using a larger round-headed brush, apply to the bottom right-hand corner in diagonal strokes, making a curve for the shoreline. With a smaller round-headed brush, mix some cream paints and loosely paint in the boat on the horizon.

4 Allow the paper to dry some more, and then paint in the sun with a combination of white, pink, orange and a speck of red. Use these same colours to add the reflective rays of the sun on the water. Finally, take your white gouache paint and use it sparingly for the white highlights of the waves. Allow to dry completely.

You will need

An A3 sheet of watercolour paper

Watercolour paints in the same colours as the painting: blues, violets, white, black, red and orange

A small tube of white gouache paint

A mixing palette

Two round-headed brushes, sizes three and four

A large square-headed brush

A sponge

Two pots of clean water

Masking tape

A board or protected tabletop to work on

A couple of sheets of kitchen roll

Top tips

• Don't worry if you can't get the same sized brushes as these; you may discover that you prefer different sizes.
• It is better to have two or three good-quality brushes than many mediocre ones.

2 Expressionism

The Expressionists were painters and sculptors mainly based in Germany during the 1920s and were heavily impacted by the terrible things they witnessed during World War I. Expressionist artists show us how they feel in their paintings – they were not interested in making exact pictures of what was in front of them.

One of the pictures in this chapter, *The Scream* by Edvard Munch, was painted before Expressionism existed as an art movement, but it influenced the Expressionists to the point that it is thought of as an Expressionist picture. Franz Marc's *Little Blue Horse* is innocent and joyful but also has a sense of fear about the future. Ernst Barlach's *The Destitution* is a dramatic woodcut that shows the awful cost of war.

The Scream

When you want to scream, inside or out, Edvard Munch's *The Scream* looks exactly the way you feel – so perfectly did Munch capture the emotional turmoil of his iconic screaming figure that his energetic style and use of colour became essential tools for the Expressionists who came after him.

What's the story?

The Scream looks like it could be a landscape anywhere, featuring anyone at all. But in fact it shows a real place, a hill called Ekeberg just outside Oslo (Norway's capital city), and the person in the picture is thought to be Edvard Munch himself.

   The Scream is also a picture of a particular moment in time. In his diary, Munch describes going for a walk with two friends at Ekeberg. He suddenly felt weak and had to stop by a fence to hold onto it and recover. His friends carried on walking without him, and while he was standing still he 'heard a huge extraordinary scream pass through nature'. Munch drew himself at the moment he experienced hearing this scream.

   Munch's original title for *The Scream* was *The Scream of Nature*. Perhaps Munch imagined a scream – one of his sisters, Laura, was mentally ill and was interned in a hospital near Ekeberg, so he may have been thinking about her when he was walking. Or perhaps Munch imagined a scream coming from the natural world all around him.

Artist	Edvard Munch
Nationality	Norwegian
Painted	1893

Think about . . .

Can anyone hear the scream?
Look at the people on the left-hand side of the picture. Are they Munch's friends? They have not turned around. They seem unaware that someone is screaming. This makes the picture even more powerful because the person in the picture is alone even though there are people nearby. Perhaps no one can hear this person scream. Perhaps the scream is silent and it is all in this person's head.

Does the background of the picture 'scream' as well?
The top third of the picture shows a sunset but the colours used are not melting golden yellows – they are hard waves of blood-like reds. The land and river beneath the sunset are drawn in swirling blacks and blues; nothing is solid and dependable – everything is constantly moving and changing. The background of the picture seems to be screaming, too.

'Is that man a ghost?'
Andrew, age 5

Project: Scream screen

Your face here

When Munch started working as an artist he was unable to afford canvas to paint on, so he used cardboard instead. When Munch became successful he carried on working on cardboard because he was used to it and liked its texture. Use cardboard to make your own version of *The Scream* in this project. Once you've finished, put your face into the hole you've cut and have someone take a picture of you as you scream like the person in Munch's picture.

You will need

A rectangle of strong cardboard – the side of a large cardboard box is ideal

A pair of scissors

A pencil

Thick crayons

1 Using your scissors, cut out a rectangle of cardboard about three times bigger than your head. Get an adult to help you if the cardboard is too tough to cut.

2 Now cut a space for your face by cutting a small oval in the middle of the cardboard. Gradually cut a bigger and bigger shape until you can just fit your face through it.

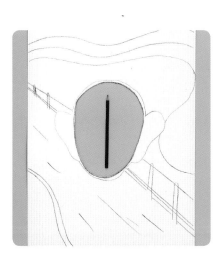

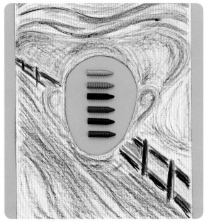

3 Using your pencil, draw a swirling landscape and sky across the cardboard.

4 Colour in the landscape with crayons. Use contrasting colours to create a dramatic effect.

Top tip

Draw a screaming face instead of cutting out a space for your face. Then cut hand holes and 'scream' through the picture with your hands instead.

Project: Screaming hair

This project shows you how to create a screaming person using coloured inks and a straw. Every time you do this project it will turn out differently.

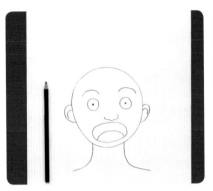

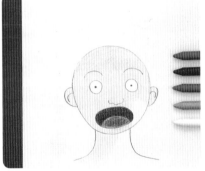

You will need

A large sheet of white paper

A pencil

Some wax crayons

Inks in two or three colours

A paintbrush

A cup of water to clean the brush

A straw

1 Use your pencil to draw an image on the paper of a person screaming. Position the head in the bottom half of the sheet of paper. Don't draw any hair on the top of the head.

2 Use wax crayons to colour in the head – the wax will resist the ink, which is useful for the next step of the project, which is making the hair.

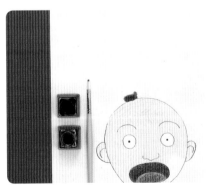

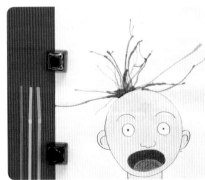

3 Blob one colour of ink onto the top of the head with your paintbrush – make it like a tiny puddle.

4 Blow through your straw onto the blob of ink to send it off in different directions. Add more colours of ink to build up a crazy head of hair.

Top tips

• Use different colours
or all the same colour to
create different effects.
• Remember to wash
the brush in between
using different colours
of ink.

Little blue horse

Horses are not blue and the earth is not bright candy-floss pink, but Franz Marc's painting *Little Blue Horse* is not about the way things look in real life – it is about how Franz Marc feels about horses and what he believes to be their spiritual essence.

Artist	Franz Marc
Nationality	German
Painted	1912

What's the story?

Franz Marc was an Expressionist painter who admired the natural world, not the world built by people and filled with machines. He painted pictures of animals because he thought that animals were innocent and beautiful and could teach human beings a lot about how to live peacefully. Marc loved horses in particular. He was aware of the history that people and horses share – since ancient times we have relied on horses to help us farm the land, transport goods and get from place to place.

In *Little Blue Horse*, what look like unrealistic colours actually stand for real emotions. Marc saw blue as a noble, strong, dominant colour – so the horse is blue. He thought that yellow was a joyful, feminine colour – so the landscape is yellow. Marc felt that red was the colour of violence – so the sky is red, indicating that danger is on the horizon.

Franz Marc fought in World War I in the German army. He was killed at the Battle of Verdun in 1916. It is thought that up to 7,000 horses were killed every day in this battle. So perhaps Marc was right about depicting the danger on the horizon.

Think about . . .

Why are the shapes in the picture so simple?
The Expressionists made the shapes – also called 'forms' – in their pictures simple because they thought that uncomplicated lines are easier to understand and represent the true essence of people, landscapes, animals and objects. They also thought that the simpler something is, the more truthful and timeless it is.

Did Marc paint other kinds of animals?
Yes, Marc admired animals of all kinds. He painted cats, deer, weasels, wolves, foxes, dogs, donkeys, monkeys, cows, lambs, pigs, tigers and gazelles – among others! He also painted animals from his imagination – mythical animals, fairy animals and fabulous animals. What is your favorite animal? Can you draw it?

'I like how bright the colours are and how they reflect off the horse's coat.'

Jason, age 10

Project: Blue hand horse

Make your own little blue horse with just your hands, some paint and a piece of paper. Like Franz Marc, create different-coloured horses, depending on how you or the horse feels.

1 Paint the bottom of your picture. This is the ground. Paint it pink, like Marc did in *Little Blue Horse*. Turn your picture upside down so that the ground is at the top of the page, as if it were the sky.

2 Position either your right or left hand on the paper so your longest fingers are touching the pink ground. Lift your hand and mark an 'x' where your palm was so you know where to place your painted handprint.

Top tips

• Make a handprint horse. Then, when it is dry, either draw and colour a background scene or cut out the horse and glue it to different backgrounds. Remember to ask permission to cut pages out of magazines before you do this.

• Make a whole herd of horses. Tape them to your bedroom wall so that they gallop across the room.

3 Paint your chosen hand all over with blue paint, using the thick paintbrush. Now make a handprint on the paper.

4 Turn your picture the right way up, with the ground at the bottom again. Wait for the paint to dry. Now paint on the horse's head, hooves, tail, mane and face.

Project: Leaping blue horse

Decorate your bedroom window with this blue, stained-glass horse.

1 Draw the outline of a horse on the blue card with your pencil or pen.

2 Cut around the horse shape with the scissors or get an adult to cut the horse shape using the craft knife.

You will need

A sheet of blue card, whatever size you want your horse to be

A pencil or pen

A pair of scissors or a craft knife

Tissue paper in different colours and patterns

A glue stick

3 Draw the shapes or patterns you want to cut out of the horse, and then cut them out with the scissors or get an adult to cut the shapes using the craft knife.

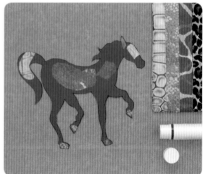

4 Trace around the borders of the cut-out shapes with the glue stick. Tear or cut pieces of tissue paper the right size to glue across the spaces on the back of the horse. Now turn your horse over and hold it up to the light for a stained-glass effect.

Top tips

• Glue on two layers of tissue paper for more 'solid' colours.

• Make a huge blue stained-glass horse to fit across a whole window or a glass door.

• Use brightly coloured tissue paper to get the most contrast between the blue cardstock and the shapes.

The Destitution

In *The Destitution*, Ernst Barlach depicts a destitute figure – someone who possibly has no home, no food, no money, no possessions, nothing. Stark, dark and emotional, his woodcut technique, popular among German Expressionists, lends itself to the picture's theme and adds to the anguish of the subject.

Artist	Ernst Barlach
Nationality	German
Painted	1918

What's the story?

Like Franz Marc, Ernst Barlach served in the German army in World War I, but unlike Marc, Barlach survived the war. He was so affected by his experience of war that his art was influenced by it for the rest of his life. Before he became a soldier Barlach had been a supporter of the war, but after he returned from the front he was a pacifist – someone who does not support violence of any kind.

The Destitution was made in 1918, which was the final year of World War I. By then most of Europe had been at war for four years, and millions of people had died, been injured, wounded, had been driven out of their homes or had lost everything. Barlach's picture could be anyone – it is hard to tell if the person in the picture is a man or a woman, German or British, French or Polish. Barlach is reminding us that nobody is safe and everyone can fall on hard times.

Think about . . .

Who are the people in the background?
The line of people in the background of *The Destitution* are probably refugees running away from the war. Refugees are people who are forced to leave their homes so that they can get away from danger. The person in the picture is so exhausted they haven't even got the energy to join the refugees as they walk by, hoping to reach safety.

Is *The Destitution* a painting?
No, *The Destitution* is a woodcut, which means that the image was cut into a block of wood. The wood was then covered in black paint, a sheet of paper was placed on top of it, and it was then pressed down to make the picture. You can make lots of versions of the same picture using a wood block.

Project: Black and white printing tile

Barlach drew *The Destitution* onto a piece of wood and then cut away
sections of the wood to make different parts of the picture stand
out. You can print your own picture by using a polystyrene tile and a
pencil instead of wood and a knife. Make your tile any size you like
and print it as many times as you like.

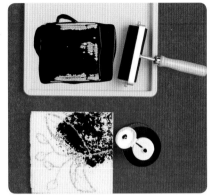

1 Create a sketch of a picture you would like to print – a picture that includes simple shapes is best. Using your pencil, draw the picture onto the tile, and then press in your design by pushing down on the polystyrene with your pencil tip.

2 Put some of the black tempera paint in the tray. Run the roller up and down the tray to coat the roller evenly with the paint. Use the roller to cover the tile with a generous layer of paint.

3 Press the tile, paint side down, onto the paper. Be sure to press the tile down firmly.

4 Recoat the tile to make a second print. Position the tile face down next to the first print. Press hard. Now lift the tile off. Do this multiple times to make a repeating pattern.

Top tips

• For the best results, make sure the tile is pressed firmly and evenly against the paper. We recommend using a spare, clean roller or a rolling pin.

• Do a couple of practice prints before doing your final print.

Project: White on black

Make a dramatic composition of glowing objects using black paper and chalk. Here we have used leaves from the garden, but you can draw anything that fits on the paper. You can also draw landscapes, seascapes and cityscapes.

1 Lay your sheet of paper down on the floor, making sure it is resting on a hard surface. Arrange your shapes on the paper and draw around the shapes with a pencil.

2 Now draw on top of the pencil line with a piece of chalk.

Top tip

Clean up any stray bits of chalk inside the line of the profile with an eraser – this will give the shapes a cleaner appearance.

3 Use your finger to push the chalk outwards from the line to create a 'halo' effect.

4 Draw around each outline with chalk a second time and smudge the chalk dust outwards again. Doing this a second time will make the shapes brighter and more solid.

You will need

A large sheet of black paper

A pencil

White chalk

Tools, kitchen utensils, leaves or interestingly shaped objects to draw

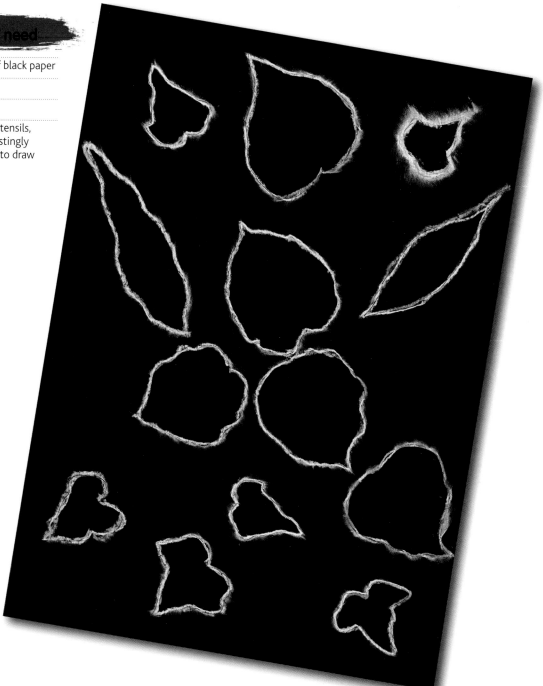

3 Portraits

The invention of photography in France in 1826 was very important for the history of art. For the first time, artists no longer had to try to paint the most realistic likeness of a person — a camera could capture exactly what a person looked like, so artists didn't have to. In the years that followed, artists reinvented portraiture and painted people, and themselves, in new and startling ways. The portraits featured in this chapter include Frida Kahlo's *Self-portrait with Small Monkey*, Pablo Picasso's *Portrait of Dora Maar* and Vincent van Gogh's *Self-portrait as a Painter*.

Self-portrait with Small Monkey

Frida Kahlo is famous for her self-portraits because they make up about one-third of her work. They show how her face changes over her lifetime, recording how she was feeling, what she was interested in, and what upset her. Kahlo's self-portraits are very honest – she was not afraid to paint herself when she was tired, ill, angry or upset.

What's the story?

Look at the monkey in Kahlo's self-portrait. Its arms are wrapped around her, and they both look out at us with thoughtful faces. Both Kahlo and the monkey wear bows in their hair of the same colour, making it look as though they got ready to have their picture painted together. The colour of the monkey's fur and Kahlo's hair is the same. It is almost as if she and the monkey are from the same family, with the monkey loving and protecting her.

There is a reason why Kahlo painted so many self-portraits. She had polio as a young child, and when she was 18, she was involved in a bus accident that left her crushed – her leg was broken in eleven places, her spine in three places, and her collarbone, ribs and pelvis were all broken as well. Somehow Kahlo survived but she was ill for the rest of her life. She spent a lot of time confined to her bed, so she had a full-length mirror fixed above her so that she could draw herself. Thanks to the mirror, even when she was unable to walk, she could paint a portrait of herself to express how she was feeling.

Artist	Frida Kahlo
Nationality	Mexican
Painted	1945

Think about. . .

Did Frida Kahlo have other pets?
Yes, as well as monkeys Kahlo kept parrots, cats, an eagle, a deer and Mexican hairless dogs, also called Xoloitzcuintli – which comes from the Aztec god Xolotl and the Aztec word for dog. The dogs were said to have mystical powers. All of these pets appeared in her paintings because she wanted to show how important they were to her.

Why did Frida Kahlo love her pets so much?
Kahlo's injuries meant that she was not able to have children. This upset her very much, and she painted pictures that showed how sad she was that she couldn't be a mother. Kahlo kept pets for company because her ill health meant she was mainly housebound, spending long hours alone. Kahlo loved her pets as if they were the children she could not have.

Project: Mirror drawing

Frida Kahlo used mirrors to help her paint. She had a mirror above her bed as an aid to drawing herself, and she used mirrors fixed to her easel to help her to draw things in her studio. Frida also held a mirror in her hand when she wanted to decorate the plaster casts she was put into to support her back. You too can use a mirror to help you draw.

1 Using the ruler and pencil, draw a straight line down the middle of your chosen picture

2 Cut the portrait in half, using your pencil line as a guide. Place one half of the picture on the left-hand side of the white paper if you are right handed, or the right-hand side if you are left-handed.

You will need

A ruler

A pencil

A pair of scissors

A portrait picture of yourself

A sheet of blank white paper

A mirror

Coloured pencils

3 Place the mirror in an upright position along the ruler line, facing the picture you have drawn. Put your nose on the top edge of the mirror. Now lean over and look in the mirror – you will see your drawing reflected in the mirror. Use this reflection to draw the other side of the picture.

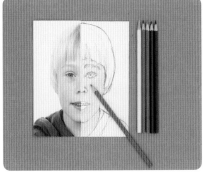

4 When you have finished drawing, take the mirror away and have a look at your picture. Colour it in – you can match up the colours with the original or you can use completely different colours.

Top tip

Use this technique to copy personal photographs or images from books and magazines, as well as drawings you have made.

Project: Animal silhouette portrait

A silhouette is an image that shows the shape and outline only of an object or person. Typically it is coloured in solid black, so it can look very striking.

1 Place your tracing paper on top of the photograph and trace the outline of the animal, using your felt-tip pen.

2 Cut out the outline on the tracing paper and place the cut-out on one of the foam sheets. Carefully cut out the silhouette from the foam sheet.

3 Apply a layer of PVA glue to the back of the silhouette, then stick this onto your background sheet, pressing down firmly.

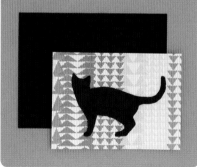

4 Place your pet portrait in the centre of the second foam sheet, making sure to leave a border. Ideally the border should be about 2.5cm (1in) on all four sides. You may need to measure and trim the edges if they are unequal.

You will need

A photograph of a pet or your favourite animal showing a side view

Tracing paper

A felt-tip pen

A pair of scissors

Two foam sheets – black or white works best

PVA glue

A contrasting background sheet – something that reminds you of the character of your pet, such as a repeated pattern of trees for a dog. This sheet should be smaller than your foam sheets and in the same format, e.g. landscape or portrait.

A ruler

Top tips

• If you can't find a background sheet you like or that reflects your pet, you can draw one.
• If you don't have a foam sheet, use stiff black or white card.

Portrait of Dora Maar

Pablo Picasso was the greatest artist of the 20th century. He worked with photography, sculpture, ceramics, murals (wall paintings), screen-printing and paintings to show the world in new ways.

Artist	Pablo Picasso
Nationality	Spanish
Painted	1939

What's the story?

This portrait is of Dora Maar, one of Picasso's girlfriends. Maar was Picasso's most influential muse for nearly a decade. Their meeting stimulated one of the most innovative periods of his career – she was, for example, the inspiration for his *Weeping Woman* series.

Picasso painted and drew Maar over and over again while they were together, and one of his portraits of her, *Dora Maar with a Cat* (1941), is one of the world's most expensive portraits – it was sold in 2006 for just over US$95 million.

Even though Picasso's portrait is a painting, it looks like a sculpture as well. The folds of the woman's dress appear to be roughly carved out of a block of stone, making her body look strong and solid. Her hair is 'carved' in the same way and is in the same colours. Everything about the woman is big – her head, eyes, lips and her nose in particular, which takes up double the space it should on her face. Look again at the woman's nose. If you look at the right-hand side of it, you can see the woman's head as a profile (side view) – or you can look at the woman's nostrils and see her face from the front as well. Whichever way you look at this portrait, from the side or the front, the woman's eyes look straight at you.

Think about. . .

Who was Dora Maar?
Maar was a poet, painter and photographer. She took photographs of street scenes and was also influenced by Surrealism. Surrealist artists painted an ordinary thing, such as a watch, and changed it in some way – for example, showing the watch melting off the side of a table.

Does the style of this picture remind you of anything else in this book?
Dora's head looks like it has been cut up and put back together again in a slightly different order. This is because this portrait of Dora Maar was influenced by Cubism, an art movement co-founded by Picasso.

Project: Cubist portrait

Make a portrait of someone that shows different sides of their head and face at the same time.

Someone who will sit still while you take their photograph

A disposable camera or a digital camera with access to a printer

A pair of scissors

A large sheet of paper

A glue stick

A large sheet of paper in the colour of your choice

A ruler

A pencil

1 Ask a friend, a brother or sister, or your mum or dad to sit for a portrait. Make sure they are comfortable and that there is plenty of light. Take lots of photos of your sitter from different angles – close up, from below and straight on.

2 Get the photos developed or print them out. Choose five of your favourite photos. Cut each one ino four or five pieces – cut in straight-lined shapes, such as triangles and squares, not circles.

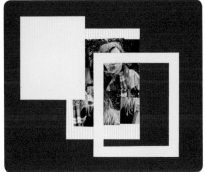

3 Try out different arrangements of your portrait pieces on the sheet of paper. Arrange the pieces so you can see your sitter's face from different viewpoints. Don't place them too close to the edges as they will be covered by the frame. When you are happy with your picture, glue the pieces down.

4 On your coloured piece of paper, measure out a border of approximately 2.5cm (1in), using a ruler and pencil. Cut out the centre part of the paper and discard. Glue your coloured border on top of your image, taking care to line up the edges of the border with the edges of the paper.

Top tips

• If you can't find someone to sit for you, choose a favourite toy to make a study of.

• Take photographs of two people. Cut up their photos and mix up the portrait pieces to make a double portrait in one.

Project: Portrait gallery

Most capital cities have a national portrait gallery, where portraits of the most important people in the nation can be seen. Make your own gallery and put portraits of people important to you in it. You will need an adult to help you with this project.

1 Paint your frame the colour you want. Leave it to dry.

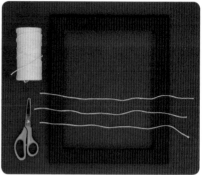

2 Hold the frame in a portrait position. Cut two or three lengths of string long enough to reach across the width of the frame, with some extra length to spare.

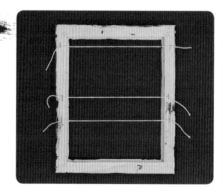

3 Flip the frame over to look at the back. Position a length of string in a straight line across the back of the frame. Hold the string tight while an adult staples the string to the frame.

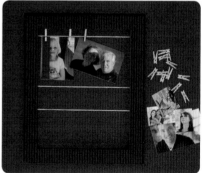

4 Repeat step 3 for all your pieces of string. Cut off any extra bits of string then turn the frame back to the front. Use the clothes pegs to clip portraits on the strings.

Self-portrait as a Painter

In this self-portrait of Vincent van Gogh, he is sitting still, but the painting looks as though it is alive – the way the paint has been put on the canvas, in thick dashes and dots of pure colour, makes the picture shimmer. The artist is motionless, but his painting pulses and vibrates.

Artist	Vincent van Gogh
Nationality	Dutch
Painted	1887–88

What's the story?

This picture was painted in Paris, where van Gogh was trying to earn a living as a painter. He thought that if he painted some good self-portraits, they might be a useful way of getting work. The painting shows van Gogh with paintbrushes, a canvas fixed to an easel and a palette loaded with paint – it is as though he is saying, 'Look at me, I'm a painter!' He has painted an advertisement for himself as an artist. Unfortunately, nobody wanted to employ van Gogh to paint their portrait, so soon after this picture was made he left Paris to live in Arles in the south of France.

In Arles, van Gogh dreamed of setting up an artists' colony – a place where artists could live and work together – and his friend and fellow artist Paul Gauguin joined him for a couple of months. But van Gogh and Gauguin argued, and Gauguin left to paint by himself. After this, van Gogh became more and more depressed, and a few years later he took his own life.

Between 1886 and his death in 1890, van Gogh painted more than 30 self-portraits. By the time he died, he had created more than 850 paintings – but he sold only one painting during his lifetime. Today his work sells for millions of pounds.

Think about. . .

Is there a name for the way van Gogh has put paint onto this canvas?
Yes, it's called impasto, which means 'dough' or 'paste' in Italian. Paint is put onto a canvas in thick strokes, giving a picture texture as well as colour.

What colours can you see on van Gogh's palette?
People who love van Gogh's work have studied the colours on the palette he holds in the picture – they are clues to how he painted. The colours include cobalt blue, white paint made of lead, dark orange, red lead, cadmium yellow, zinc yellow, chrome yellow and vermillion (red).

Project: Make an easel

An easel is useful for lots of things – you can use it to create artwork and also to display it. Here's how to make a foldaway easel out of a pizza box.

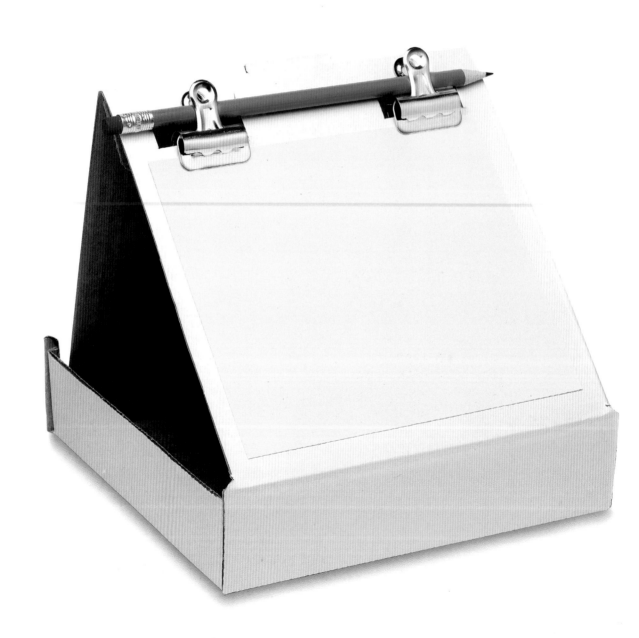

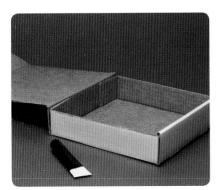

You will need

An empty pizza box

The strongest paper glue you can find

A pencil

A pair of scissors

Two bulldog clips

A square piece of corrugated cardboard that will fit exactly inside the base of the pizza box

A sheet of white paper

A heavy book to keep the easel stable

1 Open the pizza box, with the lid opened out away from you. At the back of the base of the box you will see two small flaps. Glue these to the back of the box. Glue down any other loose bits of cardboard along the walls of the base, so that the bottom of the box has four strong sides. This is the drawer of your easel.

2 At the front edge of the box lid – near where the cardboard bends down in a closing flap – mark out two narrow rectangles, slightly longer than the bulldog clips. Cut out the rectangles. Clip the bulldog clips through the holes.

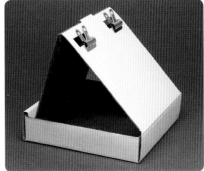

3 Line up the square of corrugated cardboard with the front of the closing flap at the front of the box lid. Glue the square on top of this front flap. This is your easel's stand.

4 Clip some paper onto the easel using the bulldog clips. Weigh down the base of your easel with something like a heavy book, to stop it from moving while you are drawing.

Top tips

• You could use clothes pegs to hold the glued cardboard walls and stand in position while they dry.

• Store art materials in the drawer of the easel when you fold it away.

Project: Swirly self-portrait background

The backgrounds of many of van Gogh's self-portraits swirl with patterns. Make a swirling background for your own self-portrait in this project, using shaving foam and paint.

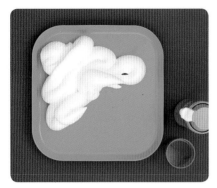

1 Squirt the shaving foam onto the tray, covering the surface.

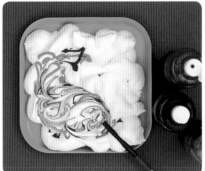

2 Squeeze or blob some acrylic paint on top of the foam. Swirl it around into different patterns with a paintbrush handle.

3 Carefully lay your white card on top of the mixture. Leave it for 30 seconds then lift it straight off. Place the card, dry side down, on a work surface and leave it for another 30 seconds, then gently wipe the mixture off the card with a sponge or cloth. The shaving foam will come off but the paint will stay. Leave the card to dry.

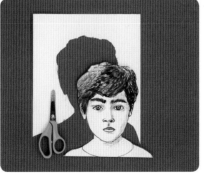

4 Cut out your self-portrait and stick it on top of the swirly background – or you could draw a portrait of yourself straight onto the background.

You will need

A tray – a baking tray or a plastic tray will work well

A can of shaving foam

Acrylic paints

Something to swirl with, such as a lolly stick, a paintbrush handle, or a fork

White construction card that fits your tray

A clean, dry sponge or cloth

A self-portrait you have drawn that will fit onto the card you are patterning or a pencil to draw on top of your background

A pair of scissors

A glue stick

Top tip

Strong colours, such as black, red and navy blue, leave darker marks on the card for a more definite pattern.

4 Abstract

In Europe and the United States, Abstract art is a
fairly recent approach to painting, only coming into
use in the last century or so. Abstract pictures don't
look like reality. Some artists who paint in an Abstract
style want to paint emotions, some want to create
an atmosphere — of calm or of energy, of movement
or of stillness — and some want to shock or challenge
the people looking at the picture. In this chapter we
look at Robert Delaunay's *Nude Woman Reading*,
Jackson Pollock's *Lavender Mist* and Piet Mondrian's
Composition with Blue and Yellow.

Nude Woman Reading

In an Abstract picture it is difficult to recognise the world around us – people, animals, objects or landscapes are not obvious or even possible to see. Robert Delaunay's picture is only half Abstract because you can see the woman at its centre – she is made up of shapes, but her upper body is quite clearly outlined. This woman is the artist's wife, Sonia, and she is sitting at a table with her back to us, reading a book. There is a mirror on the table and you can see the reflection of her face in it, but it looks like part of a rainbow rather than a face.

Artist	Robert Delaunay
Nationality	French
Painted	1920

What's the story?

This picture has been painted in the Orphism style, an art movement within Cubism pioneered by Robert and Sonia Delaunay. It focused on bringing colour and musicality to a work. All the details have been left out and the things are made up of simple shapes, such as circles and blocks. Even though Sonia Delaunay is sitting still in the picture, the room she is in seems to move and shimmer, thanks to the circles that gyrate across the surface of the painting.

The Orphists used colour to describe the world around them. Even though the colours in the picture are so bright they almost sizzle, the artist has balanced them to give the picture some depth. The bottom half of the picture contains reds, golds and yellows that are much lighter than the band of blues and purples across the top half of the picture. Using colours in this way makes it look as though Sonia is sitting in a room that is dark at the back – the tumbling circles of her golden hair stand out even more against this part of the picture. Sonia's clothes are hanging across the back of her chair and their colours balance those of the tablecloth lying under her book.

Think about. . .

Why was this art movement called Orphism?
The term *Orphism* comes from the name *Orpheus,* a Greek poet and musician who was so skilled he could hypnotise all living creatures with his music. The term was coined by a French art critic and writer called Guillaume Apollinaire. He said that the way Orphist artists used colour was so pure it was as close to music as it was possible for art to get.

What colour is missing from the picture?
Black. Look carefully – can you see any black paint? It is the one colour that Robert Delaunay avoided using.

'The blue and purple circles at the back of the room
look like a sun that's the wrong colour.'

Tilly, age 9

Project: Abstract gallery

Robert Delaunay painted three different versions of *Nude Woman Reading*. In each version of the picture he made the image more and more abstract, and brighter and brighter. Experiment with different effects and colours to make your own gallery of abstract variations.

1 Choose a picture to paint – it can be of anything, such as a family member, a pet, a pop star or a machine. Try to choose an image that is about A4 size. Photocopy the picture three times.

2 Use these photocopies to experiment with different effects and colours, painting over the basic shapes. With the first copy, try mimicking the colours and shapes but in block colour without detailing.

You will need

An A4 picture of something you want to paint

Three black-and-white copies of your chosen picture

A range of brightly coloured paints

A paintbrush

A felt-tip pen

A ruler

3 On the second copy, transform the shapes into straight lines using a ruler and felt-tip pen, and colour in your geometric shapes in whites, greys and blacks for a monochrome effect.

4 On your third copy, try using bright, outlandish colours that you wouldn't expect to find on the objects in the everyday world, and only follow the shapes loosely. Line up your three finished copies with the original and compare the different effects.

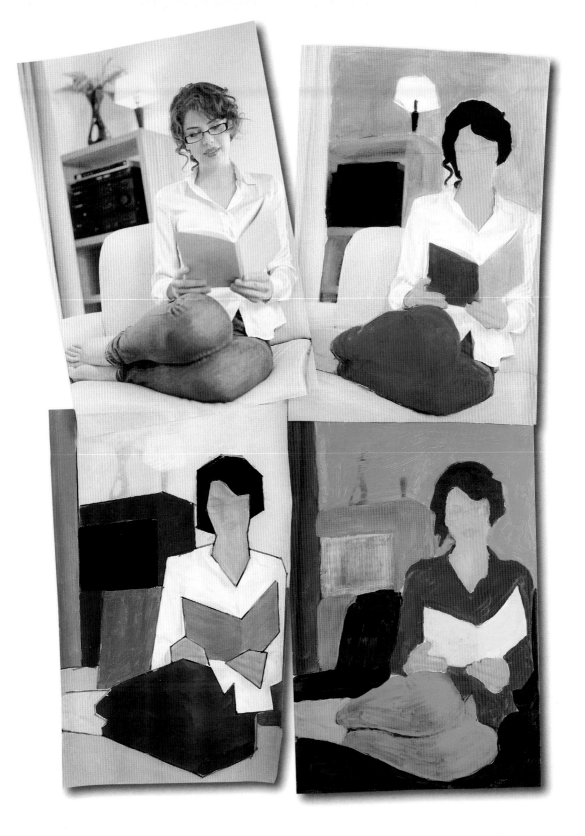

Project: Colour wheels

In this project we're going to make colour wheels, to look at the effects and differences of warm and cold colours, like those used in Delauney's picture. Colour wheels are useful as a way of organising colours, which artists can then consult to see how different colours can be mixed together or contrasted.

1 Collect together as many different-sized circles as you can find – you are going to draw around them. Cups, saucers, cookie cutters and coins are all good to use as templates.

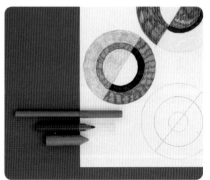

4 Fill a second circle with cold colours. Look at Delaunay's painting to see what colours he used in the colour wheels that whirl behind the woman's back.

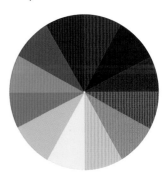

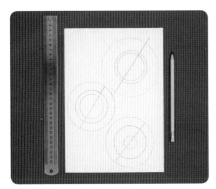

2 Draw three large circles of different sizes on your paper. Pack the circles close together. Draw smaller circles inside the large circles. Draw a straight line through the middle of each circle with your ruler.

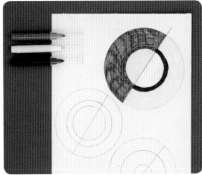

3 Fill the sections of one circle with warm colours, like reds and oranges. Use a different colour on each side of the line that halves the circle so that contrasting colours are opposite each other.

You will need

Circular objects to draw around such as plates, cups and coins

White paper

A pencil

A ruler

A range of coloured pencils, crayons or paints

This is a colour wheel. A colour wheel is divided into sections, each containing a colour. Each colour has an opposite (contrasting) colour. Colours that are opposite each other on the colour wheel are said to complement each other and colours that work in harmony with each other are side by side on the wheel.

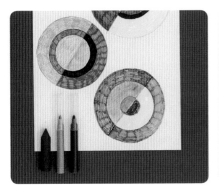

5 Fill a third circle with contrasting colours – use the colour wheel on this page as a guide – so that colours on the opposite sides of the wheel are opposite each other in your circle.

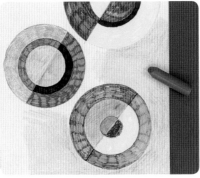

6 Fill in the background with one contrasting colour.

Lavender Mist

Jackson Pollock's painting looks like a massive slab of granite with solid patterns and black structures; it looks as if a slice has been taken out of a mountain, where the rock has been created over thousands of years. But it also seems to float on the wall like a mist – a lavender mist.

Artist	Jackson Pollock
Nationality	American
Painted	1950

What's the story?

Pollock made this picture by nailing a huge sheet of canvas to the floor of his studio. He then walked, ran and danced around the canvas, pouring, dripping, throwing and flicking paint onto it. Pollock used his hands, knives, sticks and hardened brushes to apply the paint. He splashed paint in both tiny and huge arcs so the picture had a kind of visual rhythm. When he thought it was finished, Pollock moved around it and made paint connections with a brush, retouching areas he thought needed more attention.

Unlike most artists of the time, Pollock used industrial and domestic house paints, because he liked the way they flowed out of the tin. He often mixed other things in with his paint, such as broken glass, string and sand.

People accused Pollock of making pictures that were a random mess, but if you look carefully you will see that this picture is very ordered, despite the fact that it's made up of paint drips. When Pollock created his pictures, he made decisions about where the paint would fall and controlled how it would fall – he said there were 'no accidents' in his paintings.

Pollock's Abstract paintings are not meant to look like anything in the world around us. Instead, Pollock wanted them to be images of our unconscious minds – our minds when they are daydreaming or asleep.

Think about. . .

Is there any lavender-coloured paint in this picture?
No, Pollock built up webs of salmon pink, green, white, black and brown paint over the canvas. When all these colours are placed next to each other, they give an impression of a lavender colour.

What kind of painter was Pollock?
Pollock was known as an 'action' painter because he used his whole body to paint, not just his arms, wrists, hands and eyes.

Can you see Pollock's handprints?
If you look at the top right-hand corner of the picture, you can see where the artist has put his hands in the paint and printed the canvas with them. This reminds some people of the handprints of primitive artists found next to ancient cave paintings.

'This looks like chaos to me.'

Thomas, age 11

Project: Drip a picture

See if you can 'drip' a picture. Think about the colours you are going to use – what kind of atmosphere do you want your picture to have? Do you want it to be a 'mist', like Pollock's picture? A cloud? Like the ocean? Do you want your picture to be 'noisy' or 'quiet'?

1 Take three cups and use a kebab stick to make two opposite holes about 1cm (½in) from the top of each cup. Push the kebab stick through these holes.

4 Cut open the bin liner and tape it to the floor. Place your paper on the bin liner. Make sure that the bin liner is bigger than the paper so that it protects the floor.

2 Cut a length of string and tie it to each side of the stick, outside the cup, to make a handle. Do this to all three cups. These are your swinging or dripping pots.

3 With the point of the scissors, make a hole in the bottom of each cup. Make different-sized holes in the bottom of each cup – small, medium and large.

You will need

Six disposable plastic cups

Three kebab sticks

String

A pair of scissors

A bin liner

Sticky tape

A large piece of white paper – wallpaper taped together is good

Poster paints

A large ball of molding dough to safely skewer into

5 Take the three remaining cups and squeeze some poster paint into each cup, putting a different colour in each. Add a little water to one cup, more water to another cup, and even more to the final cup.

6 Pour some paint into one of your cup-pots. Holding it by the string, set the cup swinging above the paper. Try to control the path of the paint. Experiment with colours, patterns and different thicknesses of paint.

Top tips

• Different-sized holes will give different effects. If you make the hole in the cup bigger, the paint will pour out, giving you an arc of colour. This will happen very quickly and will be difficult to control, so watch out!

• The thicker the paint, the easier it is to control the outcome, while with thinner paint you can create a finer pattern.

Project: Texture painting

Jackson Pollock added things to his paints so that when they dried, they added areas of texture that gave a different look and feel to his pictures.

1 Add a different texture to each of the four containers. Here we have used pencil sharpenings, rice, chopped-up string and lentils.

2 Add PVA glue and a different paint colour (try and make the mixture half and half) to each of the four containers, and mix well. Add more or less of something until you get the consistency you want.

3 Apply each textured paint mixture to your paper using your hands, an old spoon or a large paintbrush. Make patterns that contrast the look and feel of the textures and paint colours.

4 Leave to dry. This could take a long time, depending on what materials you have added to the paint.

Top tip

At www.jacksonpollock.org you can create your own Pollock-style painting on screen and then print it out.

Four containers

Four things to mix with the paint. You could try glitter, sand, coffee grounds, raw rice grains, string (chopped up or left long), straw or grass

A large tube of PVA glue

Poster paints – bright colours seem to work best

A sheet of paper, any colour and any size but big and thick is best

An old spoon, a large paintbrush, or you could use your hands!

Composition with Blue and Yellow

Piet Mondrian's *Composition with Blue and Yellow* is a truly Abstract painting. It is not recognisable as the natural world. Can you think of anything around you that looks this perfect or unreal? Can you think of anything that is made only of straight lines or a few colours? Perhaps something made by a computer could look like this picture, but it's hard to find something made by people that looks as pin-sharp and fault-free as this painting. The picture looks so solid it's like a piece of carpentry – it's a clean, modern construction.

Artist	Piet Mondrian
Nationality	Dutch
Painted	1935

What's the story?

Mondrian followed strict rules when he was painting. These rules were made up by a group of artists in the Netherlands in 1917. They called their group De Stijl, which means 'the Style' in Dutch, and Mondrian was an important member of De Stijl.

De Stijl artists called their art Neoplasticism. Neoplastic art does not try to copy real objects. Instead, Neoplasticism stripped painting down to bare essentials – just horizontal and vertical lines, and the primary colours red, blue and yellow, and black, white and grey. By using only these elements in their pictures, De Stijl painters thought that their pictures became 'universal', meaning that they could represent everything in the world. The De Stijl artists' use of pure colours means that their paintings look bright and fresh today, even though some of them are nearly 100 years old.

Think about. . .

Did the De Stijl artists apply their artistic rules to anything else?
Yes, they created furniture in primary colours, without curves. They published a journal to explain their theories and drew architectural plans for buildings – they even built a house according to De Stijl principles, the Rietveld Schröder House, in the Netherlands in 1924.

Was this kind of painting popular?
The De Stijl style has influenced lots of artists, graphic designers, furniture designers, architects and fashion designers.

'There aren't that many straight lines in nature so I don't understand why there are only straight lines in the picture. But I like it.'

Judith, age 12

Project: Make a Mondrian

The most difficult part of making your own Mondrian picture is making it look as perfect as possible. This method of creating the kind of picture Mondrian painted avoids messy paints, but you may need to ask an adult to help you with the straight lines.

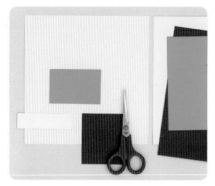

1 Using your ruler and pencil, draw, and then cut out, squares and rectangles of different sizes from the yellow, red and blue paper. Make sure all of these shapes can fit onto your white paper. Arrange them in patterns on the white paper.

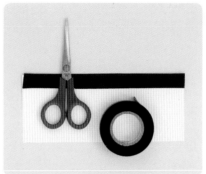

2 Tape a length of the electrical tape across the scrap paper. Cut along the edges of the tape.

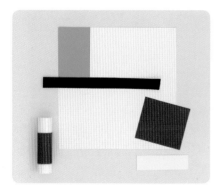

3 Use this strip to get the spaces between your coloured shapes right – check that there is enough room to fit the tape between the shapes.

4 When you are happy with your composition, stick the coloured shapes down with the glue stick. Place the tape in straight lines across your picture. Ask an adult to help you, as an extra pair of hands will make it easier to get the black lines straight.

You will need

Sheets of bright yellow paper

Sheets of bright red paper

Sheets of bright blue paper

A ruler

A pencil

A pair of scissors

A large sheet of strong white paper

A roll of black electrical tape

Some scrap paper

A glue stick

Top tip

Make an 'alternative' Mondrian. Use the same method shown here, but instead of using yellow, red and blue squares of card, use other colours, such as orange, green and purple. Stick your shapes down onto black paper and use white tape for the lines.

Project: Pocket Mondrian

This project gives you a mini-sized Mondrian to take around and show your friends. The matchbox used here doubles as both a container and a frame. You can use primary colours to match the Mondrian piece, but you can also experiment with other bright colours. It's important to try and keep the lines as straight as possible. You may find this trickier with the string than with the tape in the previous project, so take care when gluing down the string, and try to avoid getting glue on your fingers so that it sticks to the paper rather than you!

1 Take the drawer out of the matchbox cover. Paint both the drawer and the cover white all over. You might have to do a couple of coats so that the colours underneath don't show through.

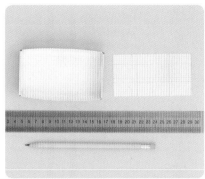

2 While the matchbox is drying, cut a piece of white paper that will fit snugly inside the drawer. Draw a Mondrian-like design onto the paper.

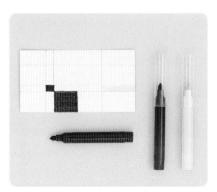

3 Colour in a selection of the blocks with felt tips, in primary colours.

4 Cut the shoelace to the same length as the pencil lines in your design. Seal the ends with PVA glue. Stick the laces down using UHU glue on the pencil lines. Use the glue stick to fix the design inside the drawer. Make sure the box sleeve is dry, then slide it on.

5 Graphic Art

The modern development of illustration as an art form really only started in the 20th century, with the arrival of mass media. Before this time it was limited to children's books and newspapers. In this chapter we look at the 19th-century English artist Aubrey Beardsley's book illustration *How Sir Bedivere Cast the Sword Excalibur into the Water* and 20th-century American graphic designer Saul Bass' movie poster *Bonjour Tristesse*.

How Sir Bedivere Cast the Sword Excalibur into the Water

This illustration is from a set that accompanied Thomas Malory's translation of *Le Morte d'Arthur* (The death of Arthur), based on the tales of King Arthur and the Knights of the Round Table. Beardsley shows his skill as a draughtsman and developed a style that was uniquely his own.

Artist	Aubrey Beardsley
Nationality	British
Painted	1893–94

What's the story?

In Beardsley's illustration of *How Sir Bedivere Cast the Sword Excalibur into the Water* we enter a dream world of timeless beauty, mystery and valour. The illustration is intricate and yet at the same time striking in its simplicity. The illustration demonstrates several influences on his work. From studying the work of Toulouse-Lautrec, Beardsley learnt effective layout and how to contrast black and white. The simplicity of the piece is inspired by his study of Japanese woodcuts whilst the dreamlike quality comes from the influence of the Pre-Raphaelite artist Edward Burne-Jones, his friend and mentor. The overall impression of the piece is one of flowing, fluid lines in a never-ending curving shape.

During the 1880s there was a shift in attitude in the arts, away from material values to spiritual ones, an exploration of the meaning of good and evil. *Le Morte d'Arthur* was therefore the perfect choice for an artist closely linked to the Aesthetic movement. Beardsley wanted to reveal the dark side of a beautiful image even to the point of the grotesque; 'I see the grotesque in everything', he once said.

The illustrations he created were inexpensive to produce and lost none of their impact on reproduction. This was one of the reasons why his work became widely recognised.

Think about. . .

How was Beardsley so influential throughout Europe despite his short life?
Through his work Beardsley captured the mood of the moment, reflecting the shift from nature to artifice. Beardsley took this one step further and emphasised the grotesque: while things may appear outwardly beautiful there was always a dark side.

Why was the subject matter of *Le Morte d'Arthur* such a good choice for Beardsley?
The stories of this book take the form of questing adventures, which explore the themes of good and evil, valour and chivalry, and spirituality. All these themes matched perfectly with Beardsley's artistic ideals.

Project: Border bookmark

The border on the Beardsley illustration is particularly
beautiful, and this is going to be the starting point for the
next project, a leather-style bookmark. In the past this style
of bookmark would have been made by impressing gold leaf
into the leather using a heated tool. Instead you are going to
use synthetic leather and gold paint applied by paintbrush
and the blunt end of a matchstick.

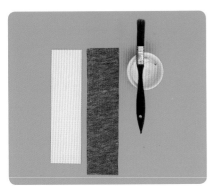

1 Glue the piece of cardboard to the back of the leather piece. Make sure you line up the two at one end only so that you leave 2cm (1in) of extra fabric at the other. This will be the fringe of the bookmark. Allow it to dry.

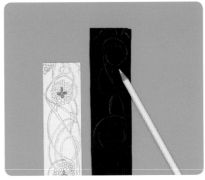

2 Use your practice sheet of paper to draw some of the designs you would like on your bookmark. When you are happy with your design, mark it out on the leather using the chinagraph pencil.

3 Pour your gold paint into the dish and then paint in the swirling stems of the bush. Allow it to dry.

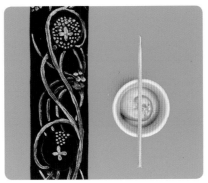

4 Dip the wood end of the matchstick into the paint and create the flower design by carefully dabbing the end of the stick onto the leather as if stamping. Allow it to dry. Fringe the end of your bookmark by making small 2cm (1in) cuts.

Top tip

You can use this technique to experiment with your own designs. Some suggestions are flowers (such as poppies, lilies and roses) and insects (such as dragonflies and butterflies).

Project: Border patterns

For this next activity you are going to recreate the intricate patterning you see in the Beardsley illustration in a simpler way, using the lace effect of a doily as a stencil. This will produce a circular Beardsley-style framing for the central image. The central image by contrast will be very simple and created using a potato print. Rather than recreating a whole scene, this just features the sword Excalibur. This project uses coloured paints, but you can also just use black to mimic Beardsley's original more closely.

1 Attach a doily (making sure it is centred) to the sheet of cartridge paper with small pieces of Blu-tack.

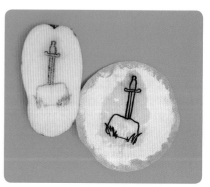

4 Ask an adult to cut your potato in half using the knife and chopping board. Trace over your drawing in black felt-tip, then press this face-down onto the potato to transfer the outline.

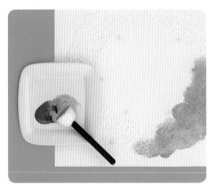

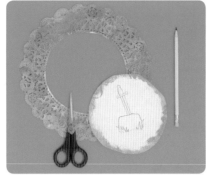

2 Put some paint onto the plate and apply it to the border of the doily using the paintbrush. When the paint is dry, lift off the doily, removing any Blu-tack. You will now have a reverse pattern of the border on your paper.

3 Cut out the centre section of the same doily and draw a simple design – here we have Excalibur set in a stone, from another part of the mythical story. Set aside the drawing.

5 Make sure you have an adult's help for this step. Using your knife, carve around the outline so the image is raised like a stamp. Then make an indented groove down the centre of the sword and across the top of the handle. Add any other detail you like at this stage; for example, here the outline of grass has been included.

6 Dip the potato in paint and practise making prints on your spare paper. When you are satisfied, press your potato print in the centre of your border pattern circle, lift and allow to dry. Your illustration is now ready to display.

Top tips

• Make sure you practise first with both the stencil painting and the potato prints.
• You could use the same border frame and then try out other designs by making a new potato print.

Bonjour Tristesse

Saul Bass' philosophy could be said to have been 'less is more'. In this film poster for the 1958 film *Bonjour Tristesse*, he uses the image of just a single teardrop to capture the bittersweet mood of the film. He is master of his medium and understands that keeping things simple creates the greatest impact and a memorable image.

Artist	Saul Bass
Nationality	American
Painted	1957

What's the story?

The poster reflects the heroine's journey from her colourful past, filled with flowers, to the black-and-white present where the raindrops turn into tears. Bass captures this bittersweet feeling of a longing for love, symbolised by the hearts in the eyes coupled with the single giant teardrop. The features are captured with a minimum of detail, using just three colours.

Bass always aimed to create an image that matched the mood and feeling of the movie. The appeal of the work lies in its apparent simplicity; everything is pared down. In fact, the first designs were considered to be too radical and simplistic by the film company so he gave them away as gifts and went on to produce more detailed designs. He developed this pared-down style from early influences of the Bauhaus and Russian Constructivism.

Other memorable images Bass designed for film posters included the spiralling eye for *Vertigo* and the zig-zagging fire escape for *West Side Story*. Whether he was creating a poster for a film or an image for a multinational company logo, he understood the importance of creating an image that people would associate with the product. As director Martin Scorsese said of him, 'He was able to create an emblematic image, instantly recognisable and immediately tied to the film.'

Think about…

Why did Bass choose to keep the design and colours so simple?
By keeping his designs simple, often using black cut-outs against a strong but limited colour palette, Bass realises that the impact is far greater and the message that the image is meant to convey is more memorable.

How would you create a film poster using the Saul Bass technique?
Think of your favourite film and consider what elements you would take from it to create a simple poster design. Experiment with different techniques like photography or printmaking to produce your poster.

Otto Preminger Presents

DEBORAH KERR DAVID NIVEN
JEAN SEBERG MYLENE DEMONGEOT
GEOFFREY HORNE in
BONJOUR TRISTESSE
JULIETTE GRECO WALTER CHIARI

with:
MARTITA HUNT ROLAND CULVER JEAN KENT DAVID OXLEY ELGA ANDERSEN SCREENPLAY BY ARTHUR LAURENTS BASED ON THE NOVEL BY FRANCOISE SAGAN
MUSIC BY GEORGES AURIC PRODUCED AND DIRECTED BY OTTO PREMINGER CINEMASCOPE TECHNICOLOR® RELEASED BY COLUMBIA PICTURES

Project: Newspaper face

For this art project you are going to be using newspaper to create a collage face like the one in the film poster. Bass would often use paper cut-outs in his work, but instead of cutting the paper, you are going to achieve the effect by tearing the paper to give softer outlines. The features are offset by the blue background and, like the original, the details have been kept to a minimum.

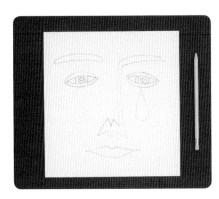

1 Using the pencil, lightly mark out the features of the face, including the giant teardrop. These will act as a guide when applying the pieces of torn newspaper.

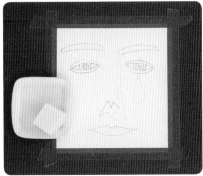

2 Tape your cartridge paper onto the board or protected tabletop. Dampen your sponge and apply it to the surface of the paper.

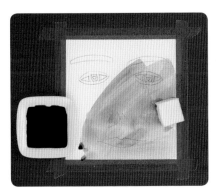

3 Now load your sponge with blue watercolour paint and spread it over the surface of the paper in broad strokes until it is completely covered. Allow to dry.

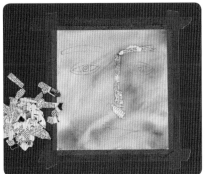

4 Tear very small pieces of newspaper and use them to fill in the features. Use solid colours for the tear and the hearts to contrast with the rest. Only apply the glue when you are happy with your arrangement.

You will need

A small piece of masking tape

A sheet of A3 white cartridge paper

An A3 board or a protected tabletop to work on

A sponge

Blue watercolour paint (the same blue as in Bass's screen print), enough to cover the sheet of cartridge paper

A pencil

A newspaper – newspaper printed on pink paper is fun, but the standard colour is fine

A pair of scissors

A glue stick

Top tips

• You may find it easier to cut out the heart shape for the eyes rather than tear them.
• If you don't have a newspaper, you could use a magazine.
• You may want to finish off your work by making a simple black frame from cardboard.

Project: Pop-eye

The key feature of the *Bonjour Tristesse* print is, of course, the teardrop, but equally impressive are the eyes, with their heart-shaped pupils and spiky eyelashes, and this is going to be the starting point for the next project. Taking the image of the eye, you are going to use it to make a printing block out of a cellulose sponge cloth. The eye print will then be printed onto blocks of colour washes of brown parcel paper in the style of Pop Art (see Chapter 6).

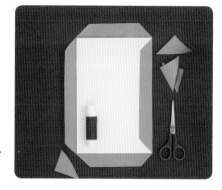

1 Position your cardboard in the middle of the reverse (matt) side of your parcel paper. Cut the corners off the paper, fold the edges over the back of the card and stick them down with glue. Turn over to the other (shiny) side, onto which you will paint.

4 Cut around the eye but ask an adult to help you cut out the centre part (what would be the white of the eye) so you are left with the heart-shaped pupil. Glue the cut-out eye onto the cork sanding block. This will act as a handle when you're printing.

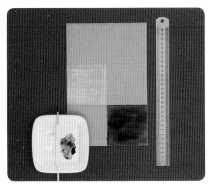

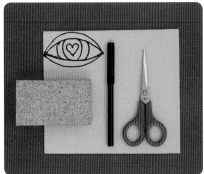

2 With your ruler, measure and mark out six squares of equal size. Now fill in each square with a different colour of watercolour paint. Use your thin brush where each square meets the next. Allow to dry.

3 With your felt-tip pen draw an eye on the sponge, including the centre but not the eyelashes. Make sure the eye is not larger than the squares on your paper, or the cork sanding block.

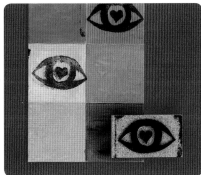

5 Pour some black poster paint into your saucer and dip your eye stamper into it. Try out the stamp on a test piece of paper.

6 When you are happy that the stamper is printing well, apply an eye print to each of the coloured squares. When dry, apply eyelashes with your felt-tip pen.

Top tip

When painting your coloured squares, paint in a random order and allow one to dry before painting more. This will avoid the colours smudging.

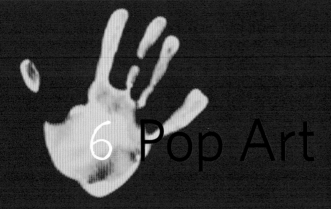

6 Pop Art

In the 1950s in the UK, artists started to see art
everywhere – on billboards, on television and on the
labels of products in shops. In the 1960s these new
ideas about art influenced artists in the United States,
and the Pop Art movement was born. Pop Art used
bright colours and big images. It depicted objects
or scenes from everyday life using commercial art
techniques (art used in advertising and selling) and
popular illustration, rather than just traditional
oil paints on canvas. Included in this chapter are
Andy Warhol's *Double Elvis* and Roy Lichtenstein's
Stepping Out.

Double Elvis

Elvis Presley was one of the most famous singers in the world – and for many people he still is, even though he died more than 30 years ago. Andy Warhol used images of celebrities and cultural icons to immortalise them as masterpieces of art.

Artist	Andy Warhol
Nationality	American
Painted	1963

What's the story?

Elvis did not come into Andy Warhol's studio and stand still, dressed as a cowboy, while Warhol painted him. Instead, Warhol used a photograph taken of Elvis when he was starring in a cowboy film as his inspiration.

The film was called *Flaming Star*, and it was made in 1960 in black and white. In the film Elvis plays a man of mixed race, with an American father and a Native American mother. He is torn between his loyalty to two different cultures. Perhaps this is why the artist made the picture a double portrait – to remind us of the different identities the character has in the film.

The portrait is made of black and silver paint on canvas, but part of it is also a silk screen (a print made by screen-printing) that has been stuck to the surface and painted over. By using black and silver paint, the artist reminds us of the black and white film photograph the picture was based on – but by using silver paint instead of white paint, Warhol has made the picture more glamourous. The double image of Elvis is like the flickering of an old-fashioned film.

Andy Warhol was one of the most famous Pop artists there has ever been. Pop artists were interested in the way that popular culture – movies, TV shows, advertising, packaging design, popular music, film stars and pop stars – and art collided, mixed and crossed over.

Think about. . .

What is Elvis shooting at?
Elvis points his gun at the people viewing the picture, but he's looking over our shoulders, making us think that something or someone is behind us, threatening us.

Why did Warhol copy a photograph?
Warhol liked to use cheap and widely available pictures from celebrity magazines, newspapers or films. He took these pictures and made them into expensive art. By doing this Warhol was asking people, 'What is art?' 'Is everything art?'

What else did Andy Warhol do?
Warhol made films, founded a magazine called *Interview*, drew magazine illustrations, made screen prints and paintings and took photographs.

Project: Double-outline portrait

Make a multiple-outline portrait with the help of some pencils, paper and tracing paper.

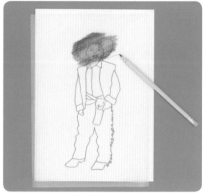

1 First find a picture of the person you want to do a double outline of – it could be a photograph of a friend or a family member. Place the tracing paper over the photo and draw the outline in felt tip.

2 Take the tracing paper off the photo and lay it, felt-tip side down, on a sheet of white paper or a white surface. Using the soft-lead pencil, shade over the felt-tip outline you can see through the tracing paper.

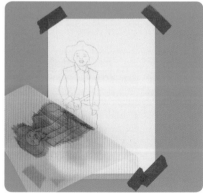

3 Take the second sheet of paper. Fix it down with masking tape. Put the tracing paper on top of the paper with the felt-tip side facing up. Use the biro to draw over the felt-tip outline. Press down hard.

4 Lift the tracing paper. The outline has been transferred to the paper below. Repeat step 3, but this time move the tracing paper to one side of the existing outline. Draw over the felt-tip outline again. Repeat as many times as you like.

You will need

A photograph for the outline

A sheet of tracing paper or greaseproof paper

A black felt-tip pen

One sheet of white paper, larger than the tracing paper

A pencil with soft lead – anything from 2B to 6B

One sheet of paper, larger than the tracing paper, any colour

Masking tape

A biro or an implement with a hard, blunt point

Top tip

Experiment with different positions for your repeat outline. You could colour in the patterns between the outlines you make.

Project: Self-portrait tile

As well as portraits in black and white or silver and black, Andy Warhol made portraits in bright colours with thick black outlines, so try using the brightest colours you can find to make your portrait pop!

1 Go over the outlines of the photocopy with the felt-tip pen, marking out the most important features. Put to one side.

4 Take the paper off to reveal the image transferred to the clay. Now cut a rectangle around your face with a ruler and cutlery knife.

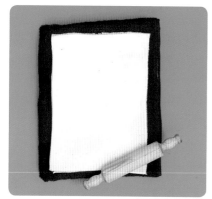

2 Lay the wet tea towel on your work surface. Put the clay on top of the tea towel and roll it out, trying to give it as even a surface as possible. Roll the clay to a thickness of about 1cm (½in) and make sure it is a little bigger than your photocopy.

3 Turn the photocopy over and put it face down on the clay. Rub the back with your hand to transfer the black pen. If it doesn't transfer it means that the clay is too dry, so spray the back of the paper with water, then rub again.

You will need

A black-and-white photocopy of a photo of yourself

A black felt-tip pen

A wet tea towel

A pack of white air-drying clay (Das is a good make)

A rolling pin

A garden water spray bottle filled with water

A ruler

A cutlery knife

A thick, clear plastic bag, e.g. a food bag, larger than your clay tile

A biro

Acrylic paints in bright colours and black

Paintbrushes

5 Place the clear plastic bag over the top of the clay and draw out your face using a biro to push down the lines. Then remove the plastic.

6 Leave the tile to dry. When it has dried, paint your face in blocks of primary colours. Apply thick black outlines over the top of the picture.

Top tips

Warhol often used colour in an unusual way, with lips painted in black or blue and faces in green or orange, so try experimenting with this as well.

Stepping Out

Look at the woman in Roy Lichtenstein's *Stepping Out* – her face is flattened and her features have shifted around in the same way that the Cubists altered the appearance of objects and people (compare it to Picasso's portrait on page 59). By copying the Cubists' style, Lichtenstein was telling us how much he admired their innovations, and the artists Pablo Picasso and Fernand Léger in particular.

Artist	Roy Lichtenstein
Nationality	American
Painted	1978

What's the story?

The couple in the painting look as though they don't quite go together. The woman's face is a mirror, and she has only one eye and a large, long curl of blonde hair. The man seems to be wearing less-modern clothes than the woman, so they might be from different periods of time.

The artist has used dots to unite the different-looking couple in the picture. These are called Benday dots and they are of equal size and different colours. They are placed close to each other, further apart or overlap to give different effects. A US illustrator and printer called Benjamin Hendry Day, Jr. invented the dots as a way of printing images quickly and cheaply. Benday dots were used in the 1950s and 1960s in comics and newspapers, which are cheap, disposable publications that people buy one day and throw away the next. Lichtenstein painstakingly painted huge canvases in comic-book style, with Benday dots in black, white and primary colours, and hung them in art galleries – where they were very expensive to buy and were definitely not thrown away.

Lichtenstein, like Warhol, was a Pop artist and he, too, chose to make art out of things that could be found everywhere in popular culture. Pop artists blurred the line between popular culture and 'high art'.

Think about

Why do you think the artist made this picture so big?
This painting is huge – it's 2 metres (7 feet) high and 1.8 metres (6 feet) wide. That's bigger than most family cars. By making a comic-book style picture so large, so epic in scale, the artist was declaring his view that it should be taken very seriously, even if the painting style is 'throw-away' and disposable, as comics and newspapers are.

Can you see any shading in the picture?
The picture is mostly made up of blocks of pure and solid colour with thick black outlines. The only place where there is any shading is on the couple's faces – and the shading is in red, not black or grey, and is made up different-sized Benday dots.

Project: Benday dot picture

In this project you will see how you can make any picture look like a Lichtenstein with this simple Benday-dot technique.

1 Draw a picture on the postcard-sized paper – something simple is best; we have copied the woman's eye from Lichtenstein's picture, with simple bold lines. Go over any pencil lines with a black marker to give the picture strong outlines.

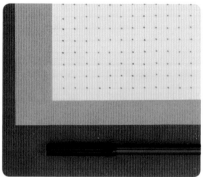

2 Place the graph paper underneath the tracing paper. Take a fine-tipped pen and mark a dot at every point where the thicker lines intersect.

A piece of white paper, postcard size

An HB pencil

A thick, black marker pen

A sheet of graph paper

A sheet of tracing paper or greaseproof paper

A fine-tipped pen

A soft-lead pencil, anything from 2B to 6B

Masking tape

A hole punch

A piece of scrap cardboard – part of a cereal packet is ideal

A biro

Felt-tip pens

An eraser

3 Turn the tracing paper over and use the soft-lead pencil to cover all of the back in graphite. Fix your picture to a work surface with masking tape. Fix the tracing sheet on top of your picture, graphite-side down, also with masking tape.

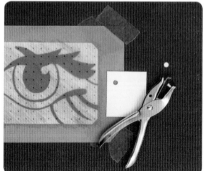

4 Using a hole punch, make a hole in the scrap cardboard. Place the card over the tracing paper. Position the hole over a pen mark, making sure the mark is right in the middle of the hole.

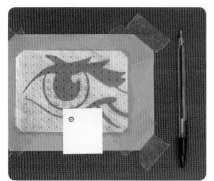

5 Using a biro, draw around the inside of the hole. This will leave the outline of a small circle on the picture underneath. Work your way along each row of pencil marks to leave rows of tiny circles on the picture underneath.

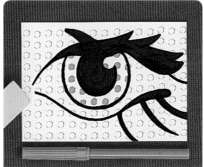

6 Remove the tracing paper. Colour in blocks of dots in bright colours. When you have finished, you can rub out any pencil marks that are left.

Top tip

Wash your hands after you have covered the back of the tracing paper in graphite – it can rub off and get everywhere.

Project: Comic cut-out box

This project uses a technique called découpage, a French term that means covering something completely in paper cut-outs and glue. It's from the French 'découper' – 'to cut out'. Choose something in your room you want to transform with a comic theme. Here, we are going to cover a small box.

1 Cut out the images you want to use from your comics – you could cut out images on a theme, such as all the images of Batman, or just cut out the images you like.

2 Using the thin glue brush, apply a thin layer of glue to the top of the box. Glue on the cut-outs. You may want to layer some images on top of each other.

3 Cover the top of the box, then cover each side. You don't have to cover the bottom and inside of the box but, if you do, wait until the outside areas of the box are dry before you do these parts.

4 Wash your hands to remove any traces of glue. Smooth out any bumps or creases in the paper with your hands. Now use the thick glue brush to cover the box with an even layer of glue – it will be white at first but when it dries it will become clear.

7 Street Art

Street Art can be found in most major cities and is created by both famous and amateur artists. Street Art grew out of graffiti, which a lot of people think of as vandalism. Street artists protest that Street Art doesn't drag down the appearance of city streets, but makes them better, more interesting places to walk and live in. Opinions on Street Art are still divided. Some cities clean Street Art off walls quickly and the only records that remain are people's photographs. Other cities ask famous Street artists to come and paint their buildings, and then they protect the pictures. In this chapter we look at Banksy's *Flower* and Roa's *Birds*.

Flower

In Banky's *Flower* a pair of double-yellow lines on a road have gone for a walk. The artist – you can see a representation of him sitting in the corner of the wall, holding his yellow-painted roller – has taken the lines over the pavement and up the wall, and they have blossomed into a huge yellow flower. Banksy is making fun of the law – double-yellow lines are a strict order from the police not to park your car in the area. At the same time, he's making people smile by turning a street in the middle of a city into a place featuring a little bit of nature.

Artist	Banksy
Nationality	British
Painted	2007

What's the story?

Street artists paint on walls, boarded-up shops, buses, trains, bus stops, bridges and street furniture such as bollards and road signs. They use different graphic techniques to paint all kinds of images – from single signatures to political statements to whole scenes that tell a story. Street artists usually work at night, while no one is looking, because their art is against the law in many countries and, in some cities, it is cleaned off walls by the authorities as soon as it appears. But in other cities, such as London, Paris, Melbourne, Berlin and New York, the work of Street artists is left alone, because their skill and sense of humour has started to be appreciated.

Banksy is a famous Street artist whose work has appeared in cities all over the world. His work now fetches hundreds of thousands of pounds at art auctions, and walls he has sprayed his images onto have been carefully taken down and sold in art galleries. In some parts of London, the authorities have started putting clear, durable covers over Banksy's work to protect it from the weather and vandalism.

Think about. . .

Who is Banksy?
No one knows for sure what he looks like, how old he is or where in the UK he was born.

How did Banksy paint the image of the artist next to the flower?
He used a stencil. A stencil is an image cut out of a piece of metal, card or plastic. You then spray or paint on top of the stencil and, when you remove it, it leaves an image below. Banksy uses stencils because they are quick. Street artists need to work quickly, in case someone comes along and stops them working.

Project: Perfect stencils

Banksy uses stencils to apply his art to walls and other surfaces. When you make a stencil, you can use it several times to make artworks that look different while using the same image over and over again.

You will need

An image you would like to make a stencil out of, like a flower or an animal

Tracing paper

A felt-tip pen

A can of spray adhesive

A piece of stiff card, about A4 size

A craft knife or scalpel

Masking tape

A sheet of paper, the same size as your stencil

Old clean sponges

Poster paints in a variety of colours

Old containers to put the paints into

1 Take a photocopy of the picture you would like to make into a stencil. Lay your tracing paper over the top and trace the basic outline using a felt-tip pen. This project will work better if you just trace the basic large shapes.

2 Ask an adult to apply spray adhesive to your piece of card and help you stick down the tracing paper on top. Ask them to cut out the shapes, following the tracing lines, using a craft knife or scalpel.

3 Using masking tape, fix your stencil on top of the sheet of paper. Dip the sponges into your chosen colours of paint and apply to the stencil.

4 Once you have finished painting, carefully peel the stencil off the paper to reveal the picture. If you want to do another stencil, perhaps in different colours of paint, wait until the stencil is dry before trying again.

Project: Muffin-case sunflowers

Make your own big, happy, yellow flower. Display it on your wall to bring a little bit of nature and Street Art into your bedroom.

1 First make the centre of your sunflower. Cut a circle the same size as the middle of the muffin cases out of the yellow card.

4 Fold the muffin cases in half to make a semicircle, fold again to make a quarter circle, and then fold one last time to get a triangular wedge shape. Draw petal shapes along the outside edge of the case and then cut out the petal shapes.

2 Cover one side of this circle with PVA glue and then lay it, glue-side down, in the sunflower seeds.

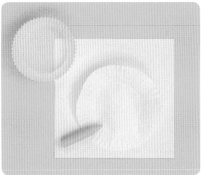

3 Now make the sunflower petals. Colour in the muffin cases with the yellow crayon. Don't colour in the middle, just the wavy edges. Pile the four muffin cases on top of each other.

You will need

A piece of yellow card

A pair of scissors

PVA glue

A saucer of sunflower seeds

Four extra-large muffin cases

A good-quality yellow crayon

A pencil

A glue stick

A green pipe cleaner

Sellotape

5 Separate the cases. With the yellow petals facing up, use the glue stick to cover the middle of one case. Stick a second case on top of the glued one, again with the yellow petals facing out, but rotate the top one slightly so that the petals aren't lying directly on top of each other.

6 Glue all the cases on top of each other in the method described in step 5. When all the cases are glued together, use the PVA glue to fix the sunflower-seed centre in place. Finally, attach the end of the pipe cleaner to the back of the flower using sellotape.

Top tips

• You can use the same technique to make other flowers: for poppies, just colour the muffin cases red and make your petal shape more rounded. For daisies, leave the petals white.

• Make all three types of flower for a bouquet for your window.

Birds

The birds on the side of this building in Austria's capital, Vienna, are so big they look as though they are about to take over the street. There's no way of avoiding art as big as this — it dominates the whole area, unlike the work of other Street artists that can be found tucked away in wall corners and under bridge arches.

Artist	Roa
Nationality	Belgian
Painted	2012

What's the story?

Roa's street art can be seen all over the world, including Russia, the Gambia in West Africa, Chile, Cambodia and the United States. He always paints massive black-and-white pictures of animals, and they are usually animals found locally in the places where he's painting. Often the animals he chooses are the ones that live side by side with people in the city and that manage to carve out a place for themselves despite the spread of the city. Sometimes Roa paints pictures of animals that have lost this fight and are skeletons or are on the way to becoming skeletons. But he sees this as a positive thing, because when one animal dies, another feeds off it to keep itself and its young alive. What Roa is really looking at is the circle of life.

Roa's paintings are extremely detailed — it's almost as if he is drawing close up on paper, not on walls with rough, uneven surfaces and windows and doors. He has to climb up ladders to spray his art onto walls, or he is lifted high in a cherry picker (a hydraulic crane with a railed platform) and has to lean out into the air to draw with household paint rollers stuck to the end of sticks. The paintings take a long time to make so Roa usually asks permission to paint them, which means his work is left in place.

Think about. . .

Why do you think the birds are all looking in different directions?
The birds are keeping watch over everybody in the neighbourhood. Only one of them, the owl, is looking out of the wall at us, the viewers. The rest are looking through people's windows and down onto the street to see what's going on.

Why do you think the only colour in the painting is in the owl's eyes?
Roa has given the owl's eyes colour because he wants to emphasise the fact that the only bird that's looking at us is the owl. Perhaps it's also because owls are thought of as wise, so he wanted to reinforce this popular belief.

'This looks so real. The birds make everything look prettier.'

Sara, age 9

Project: Big animal drawing

Use this drawing method to transfer any kind of picture and to enlarge a picture to any size.

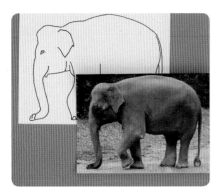

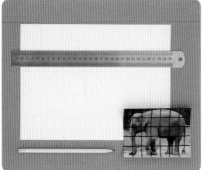

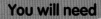
1 Choose a picture of an animal from a book. It helps if the picture is black and white. Photocopy the picture and then divide it into a grid of squares, drawn with the ruler and black pen.

2 Find a piece of paper as big as you would like your picture to be. Divide the paper into the same number of squares as your photocopy, but using a pencil this time. These squares will be much bigger than the ones on your photocopy.

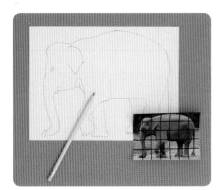

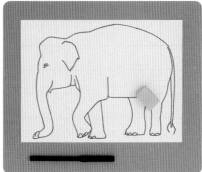

3 Look at the top left-hand square drawn on your photocopy. Draw the lines that you see there into the top left-hand square of your large piece of paper. Do this for every single square of the photocopy. You will build up an enlarged image of the original animal on the paper.

4 Go over your big drawing with a black pen. Rub out the pencil grid and all the under-drawing. Now you have the basic outline of your animal, you can start to fill it in with different shading techniques (see page 130).

Project: Shading effects

You can make a wide range of effects using only pencil. Here are some ways of using pencil to fill in a picture. We will use the animal picture we drew in the last project, but you can use any drawing you want. Use pieces of scrap paper to avoid smudging areas you have already shaded.

1 Look at your picture. Which areas should be dark and light? What kinds of textures do you want to see? Select different sections of your drawing to try out the different techniques for shading with pencil.

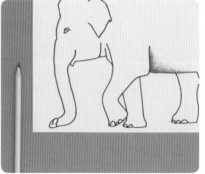

2 Dots: Small dots spaced far apart give a light texture. Heavy dots close together make an area look dark.

Top tips

• Draw with a charcoal stick or pencil on a large sheet of white paper to practise with scale.
• Draw with a white pencil on black paper to try reverse effects.
• Spray your pencil or charcoal picture with hairspray to stop it from smudging.

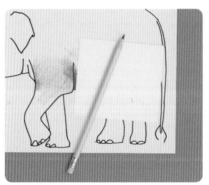

3 Cross hatching: This is when you layer straight lines on top of each other to create a shaded area. If you keep the lines far apart it looks open. Lines close together look dense. Use scrap paper to cover areas you have already shaded so that you don't smudge them with your hand.

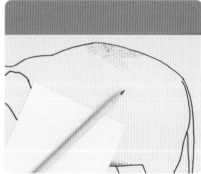

4 Dashes: Short dashes placed close together in curving lines show contours (bumps and waves). Use long dashes spaced far apart to show distance and sweeps of motion.

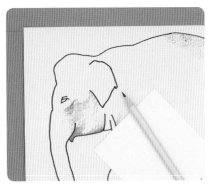

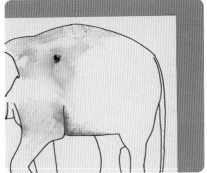

You will need

An outline drawing

An eraser

A range of pencils, anything from 4A to 6B

A piece of clean scrap paper

A putty rubber, available from art shops

5 Squiggles: Apply heavy squiggles to indicate confusion, fuzziness, fur or activity. Use light squiggles to show atmosphere, movement or hair.

6 Highlights: Use your eraser to remove spots and lines of pencil. Exposed areas are highlights. If you have a putty rubber, use it to lift off layers of graphite to create lighter areas.

Artist biographies

Banksy, birth name not confirmed

Unknown (estimated 1974)

British

There are lots of unconfirmed details about Bansky – that his birth name is Robert Banks, or possibly Robin Gunningham, that he was born in Bristol, UK, that his parents don't know what he does and think he is a painter and decorator. Other reports say that he trained as a butcher. Banksy does not appear in public to talk about his art and he has always taken care to keep his identity secret – in any photographs of him working, he covers his head with a hood and keeps his back to the camera. When Banksy paints on the streets during the day, an assistant puts up a screen for him to paint behind so that no one sees his face.

Banksy doesn't just spray his art through stencils in public spaces; he practices other art forms as well. In 2007 at the Glastonbury music festival in England, Banksy made a sculpture of Stonehenge out of portable toilets. He also paints on canvas and makes silk-screen prints, using the same methods and styles as Andy Warhol. In 2010, Banksy directed a movie, *Exit Through the Gift Shop*, which was nominated for an Oscar for Best Documentary in 2011.

Ernst Barlach

1870–1938

German

Ernst Barlach was a sculptor and writer associated with the Expressionist movement. He is most famous for his post-war sculptures, which were heavily influenced by the horrors he had seen while serving in World War I.

Barlach studied at the Royal Art School in Dresden as a student of Robert Diez, another respected German sculptor. Afterwards, Barlach worked as a sculptor, though with little financial success. A trip to Russia in 1906 proved a formative experience for Barlach in developing his own artistic style – his sculptures took on a Gothic element, with swathed figures poised in dramatic poses. He also began to emphasise the hands and faces of his subjects, bringing these aspects out in a way that would develop in his post-war work, where the faces and stances would spotlight suffering and deprivation.

Despite his initial enthusiasm for World War I, he was greatly affected by the experience; he returned from the war as a pacifist, after which his sculptures and woodcuts invariably sought to convey the suffering of humanity. The anti-war nature of his later works led to their confiscation by the Nazi Party in the lead-up to World War II.

Saul Bass

1920–1996

American

Saul Bass was an iconic graphic designer who is renowned for his work on movie-poster and logo design. He collaborated with the most famous directors of his time. Movie promotional art had, until this point, usually consisted of photographs or pictures of the stars, but Bass took a different approach, preferring instead to use abstract images, involving simple drawings and broken lettering that both advertised the feature but also hinted at the kind of story it was. He also launched a trend for filmmakers to use graphic design and animation in their credits. Bass also designed the logos for many large American companies, including Kleenex, Girl Scouts, Continental Airlines and Universal Airlines, many of which are still used today.

Aubrey Beardsley

1872–1898

British

Aubrey Beardsley was an English illustrator and author. His illustrations were drawn in black ink on a white background and were concerned with scenes from history, literature or mythology. He was a caricaturist and his paintings were often purposely grotesque, focused on the decadence of the time. Despite dying of tuberculosis at only 25 he contributed significantly to the Art Nouveau movement of the time.

Edgar Degas

1834–1917

French

Edgar Degas was a French painter regarded as a founder of Impressionism, although he preferred to be thought of as a Realist. He began as a history painter, but his style shifted to capture contemporary life instead, and he is now recognized for his depiction of movement, in particular dance.

Born in Paris, Degas began to paint from an early age. After two years of uninspiring law studies he was accepted into the École des Beaux-Arts. In 1864, Degas met Edouard Manet, who was a great influence on Degas's style. The death of his father in 1874 and the discovery of his brother's large debts meant Degas was for the first time dependent on his artwork for money; many of his greatest works date from this period.

Around this time, Degas joined a group of exhibitors who became known as the Impressionists. Degas, however, disliked the publicity around the group and struggled to get along with the others and their manner of painting outdoors, as they were mostly landscape painters like Monet. Degas remained quite an isolated figure right up until his death in Paris in 1917.

Robert Delaunay

1885–1941

French

Born in Paris, Robert Delaunay was very influenced by Impressionism and Post-Impressionism and, for a while, he painted in a style called Divisionism. Divisionist painters used blocks of colour to build up pictures of recognisable things; these blocks of colour look like pieces of mosaic. Delaunay also admired the work of the Cubists and he imitated aspects of their style too.

Gradually, from 1912 onwards, Delaunay's paintings became more and more abstract, and more and more obsessed with colour. Delaunay thought that colour was so powerful that you didn't need to paint objects, because the qualities of individual and combined colours would express enough feeling for the picture to be meaningful.

This view of the importance of colour was central to Orphism, the style of art Delaunay co-founded with his wife, Sonia. Orphism, with its focus on colour and shape, acted like a bridge between the styles of Cubism and Abstract art.

Frida Kahlo

1907–1954

Mexican

Frida Kahlo is famous for her self-portraits – of the 143 paintings of hers that survive, 55 of them are self-portraits. Kahlo's pictures can be brutally honest, showing the difficulties and disappointments of her life.

Kahlo is closely associated with Mexico, the country of her birth. She was very patriotic – she dressed in traditional Mexican clothes and campaigned for better pay and conditions for the poorest people in Mexican society. She was a member of the Communist Party and was very involved in Mexican politics. Kahlo was also known because she twice married Diego Rivera, Mexico's most successful artist. Kahlo suffered from bad health throughout her life. When she was six she caught polio, which left her with a withered right leg, and when she was 18 she was involved in a traffic accident that broke her spine. Kahlo spent long periods of time in plaster casts that encased her whole upper body and she had to undergo painful treatments that were designed to stop the bones in her spine from fusing together.

Peder Severin Kroyer

1851–1909

Danish

Born in Norway, Peder Severin Kroyer was generally regarded as the leader of a group of Danish and Nordic artists called the Skagen Painters. Like the French Impressionists, the Skagen Painters painted 'en plein air' (outdoors), and Kroyer's paintings often involved beach scenes. One of his most famous paintings, *Summer Evening on Skagen's Southern Beach with Anna Ancher and Marie Kroyer*, features his wife, Marie, who was also a painter. Kroyer regularly depicted Marie and his relationship with her in his paintings.

   Despite the strength of their initial romance in 1889, though, they divorced after six years of marriage. Kroyer suffered bouts of mental illness, and towards the end of his life, his eyesight gradually worsened, although he determinedly continued to paint until he was totally blind.

Roy Lichtenstein

1923–1997

American

Roy Lichtenstein was one of the leading painters and sculptors of the Pop Art movement in the United States. Lichtenstein was an art teacher at various universities before he became a successful artist. In 1962 his first one-man show was held in New York, and it sold out. In the exhibition Lichtenstein showed some of the images he would become famous for – large-scale adaptations of comic-strip images painted with dots just using primary colours (red, blue and yellow). The dots, called Benday dots, were used in printing technology.

   After 1966, Lichtenstein began painting his versions of famous works by artists such as van Gogh and Picasso. Lichtenstein copied these works but he made them look like his own paintings, completely different from the originals, using Benday dots, thick black outlines, and bright colours. Lichtenstein also painted abstract works, still lifes and landscapes in this style.

Franz Marc

1880–1916

German

Marc was a German Expressionist painter and a founding member of *Der Blaue Reiter Almanac*, a publication dedicated to expressing new ideas and attitudes towards modern art. Artists contributing to the almanac, such as August Macke and Wassily Kandinsky, later become known as *The Blue Rider* group. Marc liked to depict animals, and he made woodcuts and lithographs as well as paintings. His work made use of bright, primary colours, which he believed had emotional properties that communicated through the artwork. Marc was drafted into the German army during World War I and was killed in action in 1916.

Piet Mondrian

1872–1944

Dutch

Mondrian was influenced by Picasso and the Cubists, but he eventually developed his own style of painting that was very rigid and 'clean': it typically consisted of black horizontal or vertical (never diagonal) lines on a white background, filled in with some or all of the primary colours (red, blue and yellow). Mondrian called this style Neoplasticism.

The Dutch artist Theo van Doesburg founded an art movement called De Stijl (meaning 'the Style' in Dutch) in 1917. One of the most important influences on the De Stijl movement was Piet Mondrian. After seeing Mondrian's paintings in 1915, van Doesburg decided that Mondrian's work was the most perfect form of painting there was, and that everything – painting, sculpture, graphic design and architecture – should aim for the order, control and harmony of Mondrian's style. Mondrian and van Doesburg argued over the use of diagonal lines – Mondrian thought that they shouldn't be used but van Doesburg considered them to be energetic and dynamic.

Mondrian lived and worked in Paris, London and New York. He died of pneumonia in New York at the age of 71.

Claude Monet

1840–1926

French

Monet is associated with the French Impressionist movement, with the term 'Impressionism' deriving from the title of one of his paintings (*Impression, Sunrise*) shown at the first Impressionist exhibition.

Monet grew up in Le Havre, Normandy, where he became known for his caricatures before he began painting outdoors, capturing the landscapes that would later identify his work. He moved to Paris, where he met other artists, developed his artistic style, and had a son in 1867 with his future wife Camille Doncieux. They lived in poverty for a while, involving a dark period in which Monet attempted suicide. Their financial luck changed, though, when Monet secured a patron for his work. He married Camille in 1870, and she remained the model for many of his paintings. She died in 1879, after which Monet produced some of his best studies of landscapes, light and colour.

Monet eventually remarried and in 1883 moved to Giverny. He planted a large garden around his house and would often paint there; today, the house and gardens are a popular tourist destination, where the large lily-pond that formed the subject of so many of his paintings can be seen.

Edvard Munch

1853–1944

Norwegian

Munch was an Expressionist artist, whose work has been controversial – either criticised as violent and disturbing, or admired for its psychological depth. Munch initially studied engineering, but, despite his father's strong disapproval of art, he later enrolled at an art school. His relationship with his father remained tense, especially when Munch fell under the influence of his friend, the bohemian and anarchist Hans Jaeger.

Munch famously kept a 'soul diary', in order to explore his own emotions and thoughts. He was interested in the symbolic depiction of the mind, and the harsh contours that developed in his work were calculated with an engineer's precision and designed to convey vibrancy and emotion. In 1908, Munch suffered a breakdown and underwent therapy, after which his paintings became less pessimistic and were accepted

more enthusiastically by the public. Munch continued painting until his death, recording his physical deterioration through self-portraits.

Pablo Picasso

1881–1973

Spanish

Although Picasso was born in Spain, he lived most of his life in France. He was the most important artist of the 20th century, co-founding Cubism (with Georges Braque) and becoming a master of Abstract painting. Abstract paintings, which Picasso pioneered, do not try to look like real life (objects, animals, landscapes, buildings, people or things).

Picasso created art in numerous different styles as well as different materials. He designed stage sets, made and painted ceramics, experimented in photography, sculpted with many different materials (everything from bronze to parts of old bicycles), screen-printed posters, and painted murals (wall paintings) on a massive scale.

Picasso lived a long time (he died when he was 91) and worked at a furious pace right up until the end of his life, and so produced a huge amount of art.

Jackson Pollock

1912–1956

American

Jackson Pollock was an Abstract Expressionist painter, which means that he painted abstract works of art that expressed how he was feeling.

Pollock was influenced by Native American art, Mexican mural painting, Surrealism, and by the work of his wife, Lee Krasner. He created a style of painting that came to be known as 'action' painting because it was very physical – instead of standing still, painting a canvas attached to an easel, Pollock tacked huge canvases to the floor and walked around them, throwing, splashing and dripping paint onto the surface. Pollock's most famous paintings were created between 1947 and 1950, when he was totally absorbed in making his drip paintings.

Pollock numbered his paintings so that people did not come to them with any idea of what they were about or what they represented. Numbering his paintings was, as far as Pollock was concerned, another way to make them truly abstract.

Roa

Unknown

Belgian

Like the Street artist Banksy, Roa keeps his exposure to the public to a minimum. Roa paints large-scale black-and-white animals on walls and buildings. He paints out an outline of an animal in black and then fills it in with white, adding shading and highlights to the shape until he is happy with it. Very often his animals have eyes that are closed, so you don't know if they are dead or asleep.

Roa's work is known internationally, and he travels all over the world to paint. Although not much is known about him, he doesn't disguise his identity, like Banksy, and is often commissioned to paint murals.

Vincent van Gogh

1853–1890

Dutch

Vincent van Gogh was a Post-Impressionist painter, taking the ideas of the Impressionists further. He used a bolder painting style that took inspiration from the way many Japanese artists composed their pictures.

Van Gogh worked very intensely for long periods of time – in the last 10 years of his life he created more than 2,000 paintings, sketches, drawings, watercolours, and prints. Van Gogh was an idealistic young man from a very religious background, and he spent periods of time being depressed. He suffered from episodes of bad health and mental illness, particularly towards the end of his life. Eventually, unable to cope with his mental illness and lack of success as an artist, van Gogh shot himself in the chest and died of infection 29 hours later.

Almost as soon as van Gogh died, art critics, art collectors and fellow artists began to recognise his brilliance, and memorial exhibitions of his work were held all over Europe. Today, along with Picasso's, van Gogh's work is among the most sought-after modern art in the world.

Andy Warhol

1928–1977

American

Andy Warhol began his artistic life as an illustrator for magazines. He also drew advertisements for shoes and illustrated record covers. In the 1950s his work started appearing in galleries – it had made the journey from commercial art to fine art.

Warhol's beginnings as a commercial graphic artist were very important for the development of his work and for Pop Art, the movement he was part of. Pop Art took aspects of popular culture, such as advertisements, movies and food products, and represented them as art by making them into silk-screen images or sculptures.

In the 1960s Pop Art became a dominant force and Warhol's images of movie stars and other symbols of American culture, such as bottles of Coca-Cola and Campbell's soup cans, became world-famous examples of Pop Art.

Between 1962 and 1984, Warhol established three different studios in New York, which were all called the Factory. Warhol and his many assistants made artworks on a large scale at the Factory. Warhol also made movies, became involved in music, and published an influential magazine called *Interview*.

Andy Warhol survived an attempt to kill him by a fan in 1968. He died of complications from a routine operation in 1987.

Where to see the art in this book

Claude Monet, *Water-Lily Pond*, National Gallery, London, England

Edgar Degas, *Dancers at the Barre*, Phillips Collection, Washington, DC, USA

Edvard Munch, *The Scream*, Nasjonalgalleriet, Oslo, Norway

Franz Marc, *Little Blue Horse*, Saarland Museum, Saarbrucken, Germany

Frida Kahlo, *Self-portrait with Small Monkey*, Brady Museum, Cuernavaca, Mexico

Pablo Picasso, *Portrait of Dora Maar*, Reina Sofia Museum of Modern Art, Madrid, Spain

Vincent van Gogh, *Self-portrait*, Musée d'Orsay, Paris, France

Robert Delaunay, *Nude Woman Reading*, National Gallery of Victoria, Melbourne, Australia

Jackson Pollock, *Lavender Mist*, National Gallery of Art, Washington, DC, USA

Piet Mondrian, *Composition with Blue and Yellow*, Tate Gallery, London, England

Andy Warhol, *Double Elvis*, MoMA, New York, NY, USA

Roy Lichtenstein, *Stepping Out*, The Metropolitan Museum of Art, New York, NY, USA

Banksy, *Flower*, Bethnal Green, London, England

Roa, *Birds*, Vienna, Austria

The artworks not listed here are in private collections.

Glossary

A

Abstract art: A work of art that doesn't look anything like objects or people in the world. Many art movements of the 20th century were abstract, and a lot of today's art is abstract.

Abstract Expressionism: An art movement that developed in the United States in the 1940s and 1950s. Artists who paint in an Abstract Expressionist style paint abstract pictures that reflect how they feel.

action painting: A style of painting in which the paint is applied haphazardly – dripped or splashed for example – rather than methodically.

Aesthetic movement: A literary and artistic movement that flourished in England in the 1880s devoted to 'art for art's sake' and rejecting the notion that art should have a social or moral purpose.

Apollinaire, Guillaume: See Orphism.

Art Deco: A style of interior decoration, jewellery, architecture and such at its height in the 1930s and characterised by geometrical shapes and stylised natural forms.

Art Nouveau: A style of art and architecture of the 1890s, characterised by swelling, sinuous outlines and stylised natural forms, such as flowers and leaves.

avant-garde: A group of artists, musicians or writers working with new and experimental ideas and methods.

B

Bauhaus: A German school of architecture and applied arts founded in 1919 by Walter Gropius on experimental principles of functionalism and truth to materials.

broken colour: Pigment applied in broken strokes to capture the effect of light and movement.

Benday dots: Benday is a mechanical method for producing shading and stippling effects, named for the illustrator and painter, Ben Day.

C

charcoal: The name given to wood that has been burned, removing oxygen and moisture to leave carbon. The carbon looks like coal and can be used for drawing as it is, or it can be compressed into hard or soft sticks that can also be used for drawing.

collage: A way of constructing art in which the piece is assembled using different materials, objects and shapes.

colour wheel: A way of organising and displaying colours in a circle to show the variations or relationships between colours, such as primary and secondary colours, complementary and contrasting colours.

commercial art: Art used in advertising and selling.

composition: The arrangement of elements in a picture such as line, colour and form.

Constructivism: After the Russian Revolution in 1917, art in Russia changed to reflect the fact that Russian society had changed. Russian art of this time was called Constructivism, and it was aimed at ordinary people, rather than at wealthy individuals who could afford to buy expensive art by a few fashionable artists. Constructivists thought that art should not be just about itself but should be able to communicate ideas with as many people as possible. Artists within the movement, such as Rodchenko, thought that art should be put to social use and should help to make society a better place. Constructivism influenced the De Stijl art movement, among others, and also had an impact on theatre design, architecture, dance, film and industrial design.

Cubism: A style of art, especially painting, that was developed by Pablo Picasso and Georges Braque in the early 20th century. An art critic, Louis Vauxcelles, named the Cubist movement by noticing that Cubist pictures were 'full of little cubes'. In the first phase, between 1908 and 1912, Cubism showed things from lots of different angles at the same time, called Analytical Cubism. Everyday objects were broken down into basic shapes, taken apart, and put back together again in a slightly disjointed way, to represent an object from lots of different angles at the same time. The second phase was called Synthetic Cubism, active between 1912 and 1919, which used collage to depict objects and people, incorporating bits of newspapers, fabric, sheet music, magazines and books. Synthetic Cubism stuck objects together, rather than pulled them apart. After 1916 Braque worked by himself to develop his art and Picasso moved on to drawing and painting in other ways.

D

decoupage: The art of decorating an object by gluing paper cut outs onto it. From the French *découper*, which means 'to cut out.'

De Stijl: Dutch for 'the Style', this was an art movement that originated in the Netherlands in 1917 and was active until around 1931. De Stijl artists believed that art was about more than representing the world around us – it was a spiritual experience. De Stijl artists thought that the only way art could represent the spiritual was for it to mirror the harmony and order of maths – so only squares, rectangles, and horizontal and vertical straight lines were used, and only pure primary colors (red, yellow, and blue) and black and white were allowed. De Stijl art was abstract, which means it did not represent the world in a realistic way. In addition to painters there were De Stijl architects, poets, writers, and even furniture makers.

Divisionism: A style of painting characteristic of Neo-Impressionism that involved the separation of colours into individual dots which take on a different appearance from a distance.

dry brushing: Applying pigment sparsely to show the colours underneath.

E

effects de soir: The visual effect of evening light. The evening was a preferred time to paint for the Impressionists because of the exaggerated effects of light and shadow.

en plein air: To paint in the open air rather than the studio to capture the effects of light and nature directly. This was done frequently by the Impressionists.

Expressionism: An art movement mainly based in Germany during the 1920s, in which artists sought to express subjective emotions and feelings in their paintings rather than make exact pictures of what was in front of them.

F

fine art: Art that is created purely for aesthetic purposes, not for any practical use.

Futurism: An Italian art movement of the early 20th century that produced paintings, sculptures, textiles, ceramics, interior design, literature, architecture, music and industrial design. The Futurists were led by Filippo Tommaso Marinetti (1876–1944), a writer who laid out the principles of the movement in the Futurist Manifesto, first published in 1909. The Futurists hated the art of the past and were interested in all of the wonders of the modern industrial age, such as speed, machines, airplanes, cars and motorcycles. The Futurists believed that youth and violence should be praised above all the achievements of the past.

G

graffiti: Markings – words, pictures, scribbles – that are sprayed, drawn or painted onto any kind of public surface without the permission of the owners of the property, sign or structure.

grease pencil: A pencil used for marking on glossy or glazed surfaces such as glass or ceramics.

gouache: A type of paint that is densely coloured and easy to use. Unlike watercolour paints, gouache paints are not transparent (see-through) and can be mixed with other things – such as sand or chalk – to create different textures.

H

hatching: Applying a pigment in short, linear strokes of varying density.

hog hair bristle brushes: A natural bristle brush that is effective for applying heavier paints like acrylic and oil.

I

impasto: Thickly textured paint.

Impressionism: An art movement that gained prominence in the 19th century, started by a group of artists in Paris. The focus was on showing a visual impression of a particular moment – particularly the varying effects of light, colour and movement. Prominent artists within the movement included Claude Monet (1840–1926), Edouard Manet (1832–1883) and Pierre-Auguste Renoir (1841–1919). The term was first coined by art critic Louis Leroy in his review of the 1874 Impressionist exhibition, which featured Monet's painting *Impression, Sunrise*.

installation: A three-dimensional art exhibit that is constructed within a gallery or space that alters the way that space is experienced.

L

lithograph: A form of print made from lithography; a method of printing from a metal or stone surface on which the printing areas are not raised but made receptive to ink as opposed to repellent.

M

mural: Any artwork that is applied directly on to a wall.

muse: A person or animal who is a source of creative inspiration for an artist. They are often a companion to the artist. The term comes from Greek mythology – muses were the goddesses of the arts and sciences.

N

Neoplasticism: Another name for the De Stijl art movement.

O

Orphism: A movement that developed from Cubism that focused purely on the abstract and generally used bright colours. It was pioneered by Robert Delauney and his wife Sonia, and was a key step from Cubism to Abstract art. The term was coined in 1912 by Guillaume Apollinaire, a French poet and writer.

P

perspective: The skill of being able to draw or paint an object on a two-dimensional surface, such as a piece of paper, so that it looks three-dimensional. During the Renaissance, artists worked out mathematical formulas for perspective.

Pop Art: A mainly British and American art movement of the 1950s that used mass-produced popular images, such as those commonly found in advertising and commercial techniques, to make high-brow art. Famous Pop Artists include Eduardo Paolozzi (1924–2005), Peter Blake (b.1932), Andy Warhol (1928–1987), Jasper Johns (b.1930), Robert Rauschenberg (1925–2008) and Roy Lichtenstein (1923–1997).

popular illustration: A depiction of objects or scenes from everyday life rendered through commercial art techniques.

Post-Impressionism: A term that describes the style of a varied group of late 19th-century and early 20th-century artists including van Gogh, Gauguin and Cézanne. Their work developed from Impressionism, but they reacted against the naturalism of the Impressionists to explore colour, line and form, and the emotional response of the artist, a concern that led to the development of Expressionism.

Pre-Raphaelite: A brotherhood formed in 1848 as a reaction to the slick sentimentality and academic convention of much Victorian art, characterised by strong line and colour, naturalistic detail and often biblical or literary subjects. In the later movement the emphasis was on romantic, decorative depiction of classical and medieval themes.

primary colours: The three basic colours, red, yellow and blue, from which all other colours can be made but which themselves cannot be made by mixing any other colours. The combination of any two primary colours is called a secondary colour.

priming: Canvases for Impressionists and other painters were first primed in white or cream to make pigments in the painting appear lighter and brighter.

psychedelic: When referring to art, it means having intense, vivid colours or a swirling abstract pattern.

S

sgraffito: Scratching the surface layers of paint to reveal the colours underneath.

silhouette: A dark outline of an object against a lighter background.

silk screen-printing: A printing technique that traditionally used woven silk as a screen with a stencil (see stencil) fixed to it. The stencil blocks ink pushed through the silk to create a print. Silk is no longer used in silk screen-printing – now polyester is most commonly used – but the name remains.

stencil: An image cut out of a piece of metal, card or plastic that can be used to reproduce that image by applying ink or paint.

still life: A work of art that usually depicts inanimate and commonplace objects – for example, a bowl of fruit.

Street Art: Art that is developed in public places, often without official permission, such as graffiti.

Surrealism: A 20th-century avant-garde movement that placed contrasting images together in an artwork, often in a surprising or unexpected way.

W

woodcut: Woodblock prints were first created almost 2,000 years ago in China and about 700 years ago in Europe, and are still made today. One of the advantages of a cutting an image into a block is that the artists can make the same image again and again, in different colours and on different kinds of paper.

Tools of the trade

To make the most out of the activities in this book, below are listed some pointers regarding preparation and supplies:

• All of the art supplies listed in the activities in this book should be easily obtainable from supermarkets, art stores and hardware stores. However, if you are having difficulty sourcing anything, the Internet has a wealth of retailers that can deliver supplies directly to your house.

• It is advisable to cover the area in which you are working with a waterproof sheet before you start any art activity. Remember to wash your supplies and clean up your work area after the activity is over.

• It is a good idea to cover up in an old T-shirt or shirt before activities get messy.

• In general, favour good-quality materials (like brushes and paints) over poor-quality ones – you'll notice that it makes a big difference to the result of your art project and good-quality materials are typically easier to work with.

• When buying brushes for any of the painting projects featured in the book, please note that brushes are numbered according to size: the smaller the number the finer the brush.

• For media like watercolours, use two bowls of water to rinse your brushes twice so that the next colour you use is not affected by the previous colour you used.

Index

Claude Monet *Water-Lily Pond* Edgar Degas *Dancers at the Barre* Peder Severin Kroyer *Summer Evening Ska* *portrait with Small Monkey* Pablo Picasso *Portrait of Dora Maar* Vincent van Gogh *Self-portrait as a Painter* Rob Aubrey Beardsley *How Sir Bedivere Cast the Sword Excalibur into the Water* Saul Bass *Bonjour Tristesse* Andy Degas *Dancers at the Barre* Peder Severin Kroyer *Summer Evening Skagen, 1908* Edvard Munch *The Scream* Fr *Portrait of Dora Maar* Vincent van Gogh *Self-portrait as a Painter* Robert Delaunay *Nude Woman Reading* Jack *the Sword Excalibur into the Water* Saul Bass *Bonjour Tristesse* Andy Warhol *Double Elvis* Roy Lichtenstein *Ste* Kroyer *Summer Evening Skagen, 1908* Edvard Munch *The Scream* Franz Marc *Little Blue Horse* Ernst Barlach *The* *portrait as a Painter* Robert Delaunay *Nude Woman Reading* Jackson Pollock *Lavender Mist* Piet Mondrian *Cor* *Bonjour Tristesse* Andy Warhol *Double Elvis* Roy Lichtenstein *Stepping Out* Banksy *Flower* Roa *Birds* Claude M *Munch *The Scream* Franz Marc *Little Blue Horse* Ernst Barlach *The Destitution* Frida Kahlo *Self-portrait with S.* *Woman Reading* Jackson Pollock *Lavender Mist* Piet Mondrian *Composition with Blue and Yellow* Aubrey Bear* Roy Lichtenstein *Stepping Out* Banksy *Flower* Roa *Birds* Claude Monet *Water-Lily Pond* Edgar Degas *Dancers at* Ernst Barlach *The Destitution* Frida Kahlo *Self-portrait with Small Monkey* Pablo Picasso *Portrait of Dora Maar* V Mondrian *Composition with Blue and Yellow* Aubrey Beardsley *How Sir Bedivere Cast the Sword Excalibur into the* Claude Monet *Water-Lily Pond* Edgar Degas *Dancers at the Barre* Peder Severin Kroyer *Summer Evening Ska* *portrait with Small Monkey* Pablo Picasso *Portrait of Dora Maar* Vincent van Gogh *Self-portrait as a Painter* Rob Aubrey Beardsley *How Sir Bedivere Cast the Sword Excalibur into the Water* Saul Bass *Bonjour Tristesse* Andy Degas *Dancers at the Barre* Peder Severin Kroyer *Summer Evening Skagen, 1908* Edvard Munch *The Scream* Fr *Portrait of Dora Maar* Vincent van Gogh *Self-portrait as a Painter* Robert Delaunay *Nude Woman Reading* Jacks *the Sword Excalibur into the Water* Saul Bass *Bonjour Tristesse* Andy Warhol *Double Elvis* Roy Lichtenstein *Ste* Kroyer *Summer Evening Skagen, 1908* Edvard Munch *The Scream* Franz Marc *Little Blue Horse* Ernst Barlach *The* *portrait as a Painter* Robert Delaunay *Nude Woman Reading* Jackson Pollock *Lavender Mist* Piet Mondrian *Con* *Bonjour Tristesse* Andy Warhol *Double Elvis* Roy Lichtenstein *Stepping Out* Banksy *Flower* Roa *Birds* Claude M *Munch *The Scream* Franz Marc *Little Blue Horse* Ernst Barlach *The Destitution* Frida Kahlo *Self-portrait with S.* *Woman Reading* Jackson Pollock *Lavender Mist* Piet Mondrian *Composition with Blue and Yellow* Aubrey Bear* Roy Lichtenstein *Stepping Out* Banksy *Flower* Roa *Birds* Claude Monet *Water-Lily Pond* Edgar Degas *Dancers at* Ernst Barlach *The Destitution* Frida Kahlo *Self-portrait with Small Monkey* Pablo Picasso *Portrait of Dora Maar* V Mondrian *Composition with Blue and Yellow* Aubrey Beardsley *How Sir Bedivere Cast the Sword Excalibur into the* Claude Monet *Water-Lily Pond* Edgar Degas *Dancers at the Barre* Peder Severin Kroyer *Summer Evening Ska* *portrait with Small Monkey* Pablo Picasso *Portrait of Dora Maar* Vincent van Gogh *Self-portrait as a Painter* *Yellow* Aubrey Beardsley *How Sir Bedivere Cast the Sword Excalibur into the Water* Saul Bass *Bonjour Tristesse*